ADVOCACY

Court Trials ♦ Arbitrations ♦ Administrative Cases ♦ Jury Trials

OPENING AND CLOSING:
HOW TO PRESENT A CASE

By

ROGER HAYDOCK

and

JOHN SONSTENG

WEST GROUP

West's Commitment to the Environment

In 1906, West Publishing Company began recycling materials left over from the production of books. This began a tradition of efficient and responsible use of resources. Today, more than 100% of our legal books, and 75% of our college texts are printed on acid-free, recycled paper consisting of 50% new paper pulp and 50% paper that has undergone a de-inking process. We also use soy-based inks to print many of our books. West recycles nearly 22,650,000 pounds of scrap paper annually—the equivalent of 187,500 tree. Since the 1960s, West has devised ways to capture and recycle waste inks, solvents, oils, and vapors created in the printing process. We also recycle plastics of all kinds, wood, glass, corrugated cardboard, and batteries, and have eliminated the use of styrofoam book packaging. We at West are proud of the longevity and the scope of our commitment to the environment.

West pocket parts are printed on recyclable paper and can be collected and recycled with newspapers. Staples do not have to be removed because recycling companies use magnets to extract staples during the recycling process.

The cover art, reproduced with the permission of the artist, Hank Virgona, is drawn from a series entitled, *This Honorable Profession*.

Regarding his work, the artist notes:

> "The rule of law is one of the most important pillars of freedom. As an artist who frequently uses satire to make a point, I have always kept in mind the words of Thomas Jefferson: 'the price of freedom is eternal vigilance.'

> "My personal observation of the courts has shown that they are only as perfect as those who run them.

> "In graphically depicting these observations I have tried, without judgment to show this, for only through honest appraisal can we maintain the vigilance required to safeguard this most vital element of freedom."

Hank Virgona lives and works in New York City.

To: Julie

To: Michael, David, and Molly

*

ACKNOWLEDGMENTS

Many persons contributed to the making of this book. We received substantial support and assistance from our families, friends, and colleagues. We thank them all and greatly appreciate their being a part of our lives.

The students, staff, and faculty at the William Mitchell College of Law deserve special acknowledgment. Renee Anderson, Cheri Fenstermaker, and Cal Bonde greatly assisted in developing this book. Professors Peter Knapp and Ann Juergens provided us with ideas and encouragement. David Herr and other trial lawyers also provided us with suggestions and support. Aaron Dean, Renee Fast, Tiffaney George, Anne Smith, Steve Smith, and Alexandra Schaffer provided research assistance and help.

We also acknowledge those individuals in our earlier book, *Trial: Theories, Tactics, and Techniques*. The Riley v. Garfield House Apartment trial that appears in Book 5 is based on the fact pattern developed by the Association of Trial Lawyers of America. Our publisher and editors at West also deserve our deep appreciation and thanks.

We further acknowledge you who will be reading and using this book. We have written this text for you, for the clients you represent, and the system you serve.

*

PREFACE

ADVOCACY by HAYDOCK and SONSTENG consists of five books:

Book 1—Planning to Win: Effective Preparation.

Book 2—Opening and Closing: How to Present a Case

Book 3—Examining Witnesses: Direct, Cross, and Expert Examinations

Book 4—Evidence, Objections, and Exhibits

Book 5—Jury Trials

These books provide the spectrum of knowledge and skills you need to advocate a case. Each book explains the practice, rules, strategies, tactics, techniques, and theories of preparing and presenting a case. You will learn what to do, where to do it, and why to do it.

These five books explain how to be an effective advocate in all dispute resolution forums including courts, arbitrations, and administrative hearings. The materials present efficient and economical approaches to case preparation and effective approaches to trying cases before judges, jurors, arbitrators, and administrative judges. References in the text to "judges" includes judicial and administrative judges.

This series of books covers civil and criminal trials in the federal and state judicial systems, administrative proceedings, and arbitration hearings. Advocacy by Haydock and Sonsteng is the first publication of its kind to cover comprehensive advocacy skills in all these forums.

What occurs during trials, administrative cases, and arbitrations follow some common and some different rules of procedures. These materials explain both similar and differing practices. Every chapter describes alternative tactics and approaches. There is no single way to plan or present a case. Much of what occurs is determined by the advocate's approach and judgment, and examples illustrated in the text will assist you in making well-reasoned decisions.

The decisions that must be made—from the planning of what to do to the presentation of the case—are based on analytical legal reasoning and incisive judgments. Understanding how to do something and why something is done are keys to a successful case. This integrating process is a primary focus of this series of books.

Advocates make mistakes in every case, and problems commonly occur during cases. The key is not to let the mistakes and problems overwhelm or negate the presentation. Many problems can be anticipated and many mistakes can be eliminated through preparation in an understanding of available solutions described in these materials.

Ethical issues arise during the preparation and presentation of a case. An underlying premise of Advocacy by Haydock and Sonsteng is that lawyers must hold themselves to high ethical standards. An understanding of professional rules and guidelines assist in identifying ethical concerns and resolving problems.

Book One explains how to effectively, efficiently, and economically prepare and plan a case. You will learn how to be a persuasive advocate and how to tell a compelling story. You will learn how to select a case theory and develop a strategy. You will also learn how to choose a forum, select a decision maker, manage a case, anticipate problems, present evidence, identify motions, and act as an advocate. Decisions you may need to make after a case regarding post-trial and post-hearing motions and appeals are explained in case you do win and the other party cannot accept losing.

Book Two describes everything you need to know about conducting highly effective opening presentations and closing summations. Descriptions and examples of organization, structure, storytelling, persuasive approaches, improper approaches, and methods of delivery are provided. Effective ways to prepare and present a motion are also described. Did you think we were going to suggest ineffective ways?

Book Three explains all you need to effectively conduct direct and cross-examination of witnesses, including expert witnesses. The chapter on direct-examination contains strategic explanations and numerous examples of tactics and techniques that will enable you to conduct a persuasive direct examination. The chapter on cross-examination provides a complete explanation of the various types of cross-examination questions and contains numerous illustrations of successful examination approaches, including impeachment. The chapter on expert examinations provides a thorough explanation of alternative topics and questions to ask expert witnesses on direct and cross-examination. Reading this chapter will be more fun than watching Jeopardy.

Book Four comprehensively summarizes and analyzes evidentiary objections and exhibits. Specific procedures applicable to objections are explained in detail, including how to assert and pursue objections and rulings. Explanations and examples of common objections made to direct-examination and cross-examination situations are also presented. A summary compilation of the substantive rules of evidence applicable to court, arbitration, and administrative proceedings is included, including an understandable explanation of hearsay. A comprehensive chapter on exhibits provides specific explanations and examples of foundation questions necessary to introduce a variety of exhibits including common exhibits and modern demonstrative evidence. This chapter also explains the most persuasive ways to use exhibits, in an advocacy setting and at home.

Book Five explains jury selection and jury instructions. You will learn alternative theories of jury selection, how to question prospective jurors, and how to select or challenge potential jurors. You will also learn how to plan and submit jury instructions and all the rules and proceedings governing jury trials. A complete transcript of a jury trial case is included to provide you with an example of an entire jury trial from jury selection to verdict. This transcript permits you to analyze the advocacy theories, tactics, and techniques used by the attorneys, and to second and third guess them.

These books explain the whys and why nots, and the shoulds and should nots of advocacy. The chapters present numerous examples and illustrations of lawyers making presentations and examining witnesses. The examples are based on real and fictional events from the world of history, literature, art, and comedy. We selected events, parties, and witnesses that relate to the topic or skills being explained. Hopefully these illustrations will make interesting, memorable, and entertaining reading.

Our occasional attempts at humor that appear throughout the text may, with the right timing, even be funny. We often take ourselves in practice too seriously, and an occasion guffaw, moan, or snicker may help put things in proper perspective.

We hope that you are experiencing the reality of advocacy practice and its moments of adventure, frustration, excitement, challenge, and enjoyment. We encourage you to send us comments, suggestions, stories, anecdotes, and examples that we can include in our next edition. We wish you the best in being an advocate.

John Sonsteng

Roger Haydock

William Mitchell College of Law

875 Summit Avenue

St. Paul, MN 55105

February 1994

TRIAL PRACTICE TOOLS FROM WEST

Advocacy: Five Books on
   Essential Skills . . . . Haydock and Sonsteng

The Common Sense Rules
   of Trial Advocacy . . . . . . Evans

Bennett's Guide to Jury
   Selection and Trial
   Dynamics . . . . Bennett and Hirschhorn

Federal Civil Rules   Baicker-McKee, Janssen,
   Handbook . . . . Berger and Corr

Federal Practice and   Wright, Miller, Kane, Cooper,
   Procedure . . . . Marcus, Graham and Gold

The Trialbook: A Total System
   for the Preparation and
   Presentation of a Case . . . Sonsteng, Haydock and Boyd

Federal Civil Trialbook . . . . . Matthews

A Lawyer's Guide to
   Effective Negotiation
   and Mediation . . . . Lisnek

Depositions: Procedure,
   Strategy and Technique . . Lisnek and Kaufman

Handbook of Federal
   Evidence . . . . Graham

Trial Advocacy . . . . Jeans

Effective Client
   Communication: A Lawyer's
   Handbook for Interviewing
   and Counseling . . . . . . Lisnek

Photographic Evidence . . . . Scott

Federal Jury Practice
   and Instructions
   Civil and Criminal . . . . . . Devitt, Blackmar, Wolff and O'Malley

Federal Court of Appeals
   Manual . . . . Knibb

Federal Civil Judicial Procedure and Rules

Manual for Complex Litigation

Federal Rules of Evidence for United States Courts and Magistrates

WESTLAW®

Specialized Litigation Databases

AFJ	Almanac of the Federal Judiciary
AMJTA	American Journal of Trial Advocacy
BNA–PLD	BNA Products Liability Daily
CA–JI	California Jury Instructions
EXPNET	ExpertNet®
FSD	Forensic Services Directory
LITIG	Litigation
LRP–JV	Jury Verdicts and Settlement Summaries
LTG–TP	Litigation—Law Reviews, Texts and Bar Journals
MEDMAL	Medical Malpractice Lawsuit Filings
REST–TORT	Restatement of the Law—Torts
REVLITIG	The Review of Litigation
SCT–PREVIEW	Preview of U.S. Supreme Court Cases
TASA	Technical Advisory Service for Attorneys
WTH–MDML	WESTLAW Topical Highlights—Medical Malpractice
WTH–PL	WESTLAW Topical Highlights—Products Liability

Westfax®   **West CD–ROM Libraries™**   **Disk Products**

WESTLAW

The Ultimate Research System.

To order any of these trial practice tools, call your West
Representative or 1–800–328–9352.

NEED A NEW CASE RIGHT NOW?

You can get copies of new court cases faxed to you today—office,
courthouse or hotel, anywhere a fax machine is available. Call
WEST*fax* at 1–800–562–2329.

June 1994

BOOK TWO
OPENING AND CLOSING: HOW TO PRESENT A CASE

TABLE OF CONTENTS

BOOK TWO
OPENING AND CLOSING: HOW TO PRESENT A CASE

ANALYSIS OF SECTIONS

CHAPTER 1. MOTION PRACTICE

CHAPTER 2. OPENING PRESENTATIONS

CHAPTER 3. SUMMATION

INTRODUCTION

This book covers the making of presentations in a case. Chapter One explains the preparation of and effective presentation of motions. Chapter Two describes how to prepare for and present an opening statement effectively, including how to tell and deliver a persuasive story. Chapter Three explains how to prepare, organize, present, and deliver an effective summation. These skills are essential to your being a successful advocate because they . . . well, read this chapter.

*

CHAPTER 1
MOTION PRACTICE

A. HOW TO PREPARE FOR A MOTION
ARGUMENT

1.01 Will There be Oral Argument?

In many administrative hearings and arbitrations, the motion or request are decided based on the written submissions of the parties and without oral argument. Parties may request an opportunity for oral argument. In litigation, parties commonly have a right to oral argument before a final decision is made. In many jurisdictions, a judge may advise the parties of a tentatively ruling based on the written submissions and permit the parties an opportunity to present arguments relating to the tentative ruling and its reasoning. Parties may choose not to argue and to accept the tentative ruling.

The following sections provides suggestions for oral arguments supporting or opposing motions and requests.

1.02 How Much Time Will Be Available?

Whether a specific time limit will be set for a motion argument depends upon the judge. Some judges schedule motions for a specific and limited amount of time; other judges schedule motions in sequence and allow attorneys a reasonable time for argument. The amount of time allocated depends on the importance of the motion, the length of the case, and how much time the judge can devote to the entire case. The advocate must decide how much time is necessary and how the available time should be used. If more time for argument is needed than is allocated, the advocate may contact administrative personnel to request additional time, or just keep talking and wait for the judge's gavel to fall.

1.03 How Prepared is the Decision Maker?

An advocate must ascertain whether the judge has read or is familiar with the motion, the case, and the applicable law. Some judges review the file before the hearing; others do not have time to do so. The extent of the judge's familiarity with the motion determines the content of the motion argument. If a judge is not familiar with the motion, then the advocate must inform the judge about the motion. Otherwise, the judge may spend the first few minutes looking through the file rather than listening to the beginning of the attorney's argument. A judge who is familiar with the case may not need much background information about the case. The extent of a judge's preparation may be learned from experience, by contacting the clerk and inquiring about the judge's knowledge of the case, or by simply (and diplomatically) asking the judge if the judge had the opportunity to review the file and motion.

1.04 Supporting Memorandum

Some forums require that a memorandum or citation of authorities be submitted in support of a motion. Motion memoranda are usually submitted prior to the oral motion argument, but may also be submitted after the argument if some issues were raised during argument which need briefing to assist the judge in making a decision. An advocate may also suggest that a memorandum and reply be submitted, or a judge may request such submissions from the attorneys.

A memorandum should be short and contain a summary of the vital facts and the legal authorities supporting the position asserted by the attorney. A lengthy, detailed memorandum is usually unnecessary for a motion argument because most judges, due to crowded calendars and for reasons of efficiency, will not be able to read such a memorandum thoroughly. A short memorandum that identifies the issues and supporting legal authorities and citations or highlighted copies of judicial and administrative opinions, statutes, regulations or rules may be sufficient.

1.05 Opposing Memorandum

Submitting a written memorandum in opposition to a motion is required in many forums and expected in many others. An opposing memorandum must explain why the motion should be denied. An effective reply memorandum should address and refute arguments made in the opponent's motion memorandum. This review of the other side's statements should focus on revealing weaknesses and mistakes such as factual misstatements or omissions, legal errors, inadequately supported legal or factual conclusions, inappropriate issues, illogical arguments, inconsistent positions, and concessions. An opposing memorandum need not be submitted in all situations. Some positions advanced by the other side deserve no rebuttal while others may be rebutted adequately during oral argument.

1.06 Location

Motions are argued in the judge's chambers or in the court or hearing room. Some judges may prefer to discuss the merits of the motion on an informal basis in the chambers, where the advocates and the judge are seated around the judge's desk or a conference table. Other judges may prefer the formality of a court or hearing room. For presentation of a motion in a courtroom, the advocate usually stands and argues before the judge, who sits at the bench. If the presentation of the argument or the determination of the judge would be enhanced by arguing the motion in either the chambers or the court or hearing room, the advocate should make that request of the judge. Suggesting the hearing be held in the advocate's office may be a bit too progressive an idea.

1.07 Sequence

The moving party usually argues first. Then the opponent is given an opportunity to speak in opposition to the motion. Judges ordinarily permit rebuttal arguments by both sides as long as the statements are responsive and not repetitious.

1.08 Recording

The practice of recording oral arguments varies among forums and judges. There may be no reason for the argument to be recorded. In such instances, the advocate need not be concerned with the making of a record. But if the advocate wants a record made, the presence of a reporter should be requested.

The making of a record usually influences the tenor and content of statements made by the advocates and the judge, and reduces the likelihood that injudicious or extraneous statements will be made. A record preserves everything that is requested and argued and everything that is decided by the judge. Further, a transcript can be used to present grounds for a new trial motion or an appeal and can be made available for a client who is not present. An alternative to having the reporter present to record the entire motion argument is to argue the motion off the record and then summarize the motion and the relief sought and have the judge explain the ruling on the record.

B. HOW TO PRESENT A MOTION EFFECTIVELY

Oral motion argument techniques do not differ significantly from other oral argument situations. An effective, efficient, and economical presentation in support of or in opposition to a motion must address the following question: What information does the decision maker need to decide the motion in favor of the client? After determining this information, the attorney must then present the information persuasively. The appropriate techniques to be employed depend upon the decision maker's familiarity and experience with the motion, the type of motion presented, the position asserted by the opponent, and the time available.

1.09 Be Brief

Be brief!

1.10 Communicate

Many advocates present motion arguments in a formal manner, as if they were in a debate. This approach may not be as effective as a conversational approach in which the advocate converses with the decision maker instead of presenting an argument. To be an effective "conversationalist" in this setting, the advocate must adopt a persuasive style, display familiarity with the facts and the law, demonstrate confidence, and persist when necessary. Rapport, eye contact, voice tone, diction, pace, and gestures are among the many factors which influence the effectiveness of a presentation. Minimally, reasonable efforts should be made to keep the decision maker awake.

1.11 Be Orderly

The substance of an argument should be prefaced with a brief outline of what will be covered. This expansion will make the argument easier to follow and understand. The decision maker may then suggest certain matters need not be covered, and may be inclined to postpone asking questions about a matter until that point is reached during the argument.

The advocate who speaks first may also want to include as an introductory reminder a short description of the motion, its grounds, and the relief sought. The advocate may also wish to provide some background regarding the nature and history of the case in order to put the motion in perspective. An opponent may provide such information if the moving party fails to do so.

The argument must be structured in an effective, persuasive manner. The optimum order for an argument depends on the type of motion presented. Any lengthy argument must be carefully structured so that it can be easily followed. The motion, memorandum, proposed order, affidavits, or other motion papers may provide an outline for structuring the argument.

1.12 Have Substance

What an advocate says and what relief is requested depends upon the type of motion presented. The presentation should contain an explanation of the facts and the law mixed with reason, logic, emotion, and equity. Considerations that increase the persuasive value of an argument should be reviewed, including:

Is the motion a common, routine request or an unusual request?

Should the strongest position be asserted first, with the second strongest position last and other, weaker positions explained in between?

Should key words, phrases, or positions be emphasized and repeated throughout the argument?

Should the circumstances causing the motion to be brought be mentioned?

Should the failure or refusal of the opposing attorney to cooperate with the moving attorney in resolving or compromising the issues of the motion be mentioned?

Should the advocate pout? Cry?

1.13   Explain the Law

Legal explanations should be accurate and understandable. Many arguments lose their effectiveness because the applicable law is exaggerated or explained in a confusing way. An advocate should carefully select the references to the law to be explained during argument. Leading cases, supporting statutes and regulations, and persuasive quotations should be used when necessary. Cases from other jurisdictions, peripheral legal authorities, and overly technical explanations should be avoided. Legal matters should be argued if they can be explained more effectively in oral argument than in a brief. Legal matters which may be effectively presented in a memorandum need not be repeated orally, unless the attorney anticipates the decision maker will not carefully read the memorandum, or unless the arguments need clarification.

References to the law should also be concise. Quotations from cases or statutes should be woven into an argument and should not be read at length. Long quotes and specific citations should be provided in a memorandum, brief or outline of authorities.

1.14   Describe The Facts

Many motions revolve around questions of law and the facts of the case may not make a significant difference in the outcome of the motion. Other motions depend upon the development of the facts. Facts in a motion hearing are often presented by submitting affidavits which contain the relevant and necessary information. Some motion hearings involve the presentation of live testimony through witnesses and the introduction of exhibits. Such evidence offered during a motion hearing usually mirrors the direct and cross-examinations of the witnesses in a trial or hearing.

1.15 Be Descriptive

A description of the facts should include a complete and accurate recitation of the relevant evidence. Some advocates tend to ramble during motion arguments, providing factual information not appearing in an affidavit, in the file, or in the record. An opposing advocate should point out the inadequacy of this information and the inappropriateness of an advocate attempting to testify or provide evidence in an improper manner. Other advocates may exaggerate or stretch the facts to match a point of law. These tactics usually backfire because the inherent weakness of such positions are readily apparent.

1.16 Use Notes

Arguments should not be read. Notes outlining the essential points of an argument may be used as a guide during a presentation. A lack of notes may indicate a lack of preparation by an attorney and may make a complete and logical presentation difficult. The use of notes, however, should not detract from the presentation of the argument. Advocates should be flexible and not "glued" to their notes because the decision maker may interrupt and direct the argument to other issues not anticipated in the notes. The advocate must be so well prepared that interruptions and questions do not fluster, confuse, or cause the advocate to faint.

1.17 Use Exhibits

Exhibits, including real and demonstrative evidence, or visual aids such as diagrams, charts, and graphs may assist an attorney's presentation, and may help the decision maker understand an argument. The use of these exhibits should be used if they enhance the persuasiveness of an argument, but not, obviously, if they prolong or confuse the argument.

1.18 Avoid Interruptions

An advocate should avoid interrupting an opponent or the decision maker. Interrupting is unprofessional and discourteous, unless the opponent's statements are unfairly prejudicial, bear no relation to the motion, or mischaracterize something that requires immediate correction. A more effective approach is to note any misstatements of fact or law and comment on them after the opponent has completed an argument.

An advocate should direct all statements to the decision maker, should avoid arguing directly with the opponent, and should refrain from suggesting alternative career options for the other side. Some situations may require that an advocate request that the opponent be admonished for making disparaging statements, or direct the opponent to apologize for a remark.

1.19 Explore Weaknesses

An argument should contain references to the weaknesses of the opponent's case or to the inappropriateness of a position taken by the other side. This requires an advocate to anticipate positions taken by an opponent and counter those points during the argument. If this is not possible or appropriate, rebuttal will afford an opportunity to expose the weakness in the opponent's case. An argument sounds more persuasive if made in a positive, constructive manner. A defensive argument that merely attacks the opposition appears weak.

1.20 Be Candid

An advocate must be candid during an argument. If the facts and supporting law provide a moving party with a reasonable position, an opponent should not unnecessarily criticize the position or pretend that precedent mandates otherwise.

An advocate may also have to compromise during a motion hearing. The hearing may be an opportunity to negotiate a resolution to the problem. Advocates who maintain set positions during a motion hearing must be prepared to propose or accept alternative positions to resolve a matter. A motion hearing may provide a forum for the decision maker to mediate a solution to a problem the advocates were unable to resolve on their own.

1.21 Answer Questions

Questions asked by the decision maker should be answered at the time asked. Rarely should answers be postponed. An advocate should answer questions directly and completely and should avoid being evasive, but should admit to not knowing an answer, if the answer is unknown. Efforts should be made to provide answers in a light most favorable to the client's position. An advocate must be prepared, if necessary, to concede a point in a response to avoid arguing an issue. Any concession should be put in perspective, and the advocate should continue on with another point.

Questions should be encouraged. An advocate may want to ask if the decision maker has any questions. It is critical to address and resolve the issues the decision maker is considering, and an effective way to determine the issues is to ask.

1.22 Involve the Decision Maker

The argument should be prepared and presented in such a way as to involve the decision maker in the motion. Some are inclined to be active while others are more inclined to be passive during oral argument. An effective presentation often develops an interchange between the advocate and the decision maker.

1.23 Brace Yourself

After hearing arguments on a motion, the decision maker makes the ruling orally or in writing. Few point their thumb up or down to signal their rulings. If a proposed order has been submitted, that may be signed. In litigation, the rulings and orders made during a case are interlocutory orders and are appealable along with the final judgment entered in the case. A few rulings or orders, which involve significant issues dispositive of a case, may be immediately appealable.

The determination whether to grant or deny the motion is not always based on the law and the facts of the case. Other considerations may influence the decision. Some decision makers believe that a case ought to be settled, and realize that if a motion is decided in a certain way, settlement will be more likely to occur. Others believe that one party has a much stronger case than the other party and rule on a motion to increase the chances that the party with the stronger case will prevail. Motions may provide an opportunity for a decision maker to influence the result of a case, and some take advantage of this opportunity.

*

CHAPTER 2 OPENING PRESENTATIONS

Let us watch our beginnings, and results will manage themselves.

— Alexander Clark

A. SCOPE

2.01 Why Open?

The opening statement provides the attorney with the opportunity to explain the evidence and to describe the issues to be presented. An opening statement can have a significant impact on the initial understanding and impression of the case. Surveys have established that fact finders often decide consistently with the early positions formed during the opening statement. While a final result will be affected by other events such as the effective introduction of evidence, credible witnesses, or a persuasive closing statement, the more effective an opening statement is, the more likely a favorable decision will be obtained.

The purposes of an opening statement are:

    To explain the evidence to the fact finder.

    To tell an interesting and compelling story.

    To explain what the case is all about including theories, issues, claims, defenses, and positions.

    To persuade the fact finder of the merits of the case.

    To motivate the fact finder to want to render a favorable verdict.

2.02 What to Say

An opening statement presents facts and opinions which will be introduced as evidence. The facts that can be described include direct and circumstantial evidence and reasonable inferences drawn from this evidence. The opinions that can be described include admissible lay and expert opinions.

The goal is to tell a story about the evidence. Any admissible evidence, even if in dispute, can be presented. The advocate can refer to evidence from any source, including evidence introduced by opposing counsel. Not all evidence will be referred to during the opening. A skilled advocate selects significant facts and opinions that meet the purposes of an effective opening without including all details of the case or insignificant information.

2.03 What Not to Say

One conservative "test" to determine whether an attorney can explain facts and opinions during opening is to determine whether a witness, a document or some other form of evidence will provide such information. If the answer is yes, the statement may be made during the opening; if no, then that statement is probably inappropriate and objectionable. Adherence to this conservative test minimizes objections to an opening statement. Strict adherence, however, may deprive an opening statement of the persuasive impact needed to be most effective, including an appropriate explanation of the case theory.

2.04 Include Theories and Issues

The theme and theories developed in case preparation should be presented in the opening. They are the basis for the presentation of evidence and when clearly developed in the opening as a part of what will be proved they provide a structure for the evidence.

2.05 Explain the Appropriate Law

In a bench trial, arbitration, and administrative hearing, the advocate can ordinarily discuss the law and explain legal issues. In a jury trial, the judge explains the law to the jury, and the attorney may make short, accurate references about the law. An advocate can concisely refer to the legal issues in the case, the elements that comprise a claim or defense, and the burden of proof. An advocate can also show how the facts establish the issues, prove the elements, and meet the burden of proof.

2.06 Why Argue?

The general rule is that it is improper to present arguments during an opening. The advocate should present the most persuasive opening possible, and a skilled advocate attempts to present an opening statement that touches the line of argument but does not cross over that line. There is often a fine line between what is improper argument and what may be stated during an opening statement. Advocates have more flexibility and freedom in opening statements before judges, arbitrators, and administrative hearing officers. Attorneys are more restricted in jury trial opening statements.

B. HOW TO PREPARE

The preparation of an opening statement includes the selection of the evidence to be explained, the themes and theories to be described, the law to be explained, the most effective way to present the information, and additional planning considerations discussed in this section.

2.07 What About Preliminary Evidentiary Rulings?

When determining what to present during the opening statement, the attorney must ascertain whether an in limine ruling is necessary before talking about questionable evidence. An opening statement may not refer to evidence that is inadmissible. Preliminary evidentiary rulings permit the advocate to plan an opening statement knowing what evidence will be admissible. An attorney may want to obtain an advance ruling to avoid an objection by the opposing lawyer to questionable evidence. An opposing attorney may also want to obtain a ruling to prevent a fact finder from initially considering evidence that will not be admissible.

Not all evidentiary problems will be resolved in advance. A ruling may be deferred on admissibility until the evidence is actually introduced. An advocate may decide not to seek an advance ruling for tactical reasons. An attorney may prefer to assume the evidence will be admissible, or may not want to suggest that some evidence might be objectionable. In these and other situations the attorney may need to plan the opening statement without the benefit of an advance ruling, and without knowing exactly what evidence will be admitted.

2.08 What Has Happened?

An opening statement should be based in part on what has happened previously. Prehearing discussions with a judge, arbitrator or hearing officer will affect the content and detail of an opening statement to that same person sitting as a fact finder. Remarks made during jury selection and during preliminary instructions by the judge to the jury may affect what should be said and how it should be said during opening.

2.09 How Will You Close?

The final argument constitutes the foundation for the opening statement. If a fact, opinion, theory, issue, or position is not going to be a part of the closing statement, it should not be part of the opening statement or the rest of the case. The opening statement must be consistent with what will be presented in summation.

2.10 What Will Your Opponent Say?

When preparing an opening statement, an attorney needs to review the case from the perspective of the opposition. The advocate must anticipate and attempt to diffuse the other side's opening statement, theories, evidence, and case. The more accurately an attorney anticipates the other side's positions, the more effective the attorney can be in presenting an opening statement that diminishes the effect of what the other side has said or will say.

2.11 Select Some Visual Aids and Exhibits

An attorney must decide whether to use visual aids or exhibits during the opening statement. Consideration should be given to the persuasive impact these devices may have and how they will make the opening statement more understandable and interesting.

2.12 Who Opens When?

The general rule is that the party with the burden of proof gives the first opening statement. A plaintiff/prosecutor has the burden of proof in a case and makes the first opening. The defendant then has an opportunity to present an opening immediately after the plaintiff/prosecutor has completed the initial opening. The defense may also have the option of delaying the opening until after the plaintiff/prosecutor has presented evidence and rested. In cases with multiple plaintiffs or defendants, the order of the opening statements is determined based on one or more of the following factors: which plaintiff has the more substantial burden of proof, the chronology of the factual events, which defendant has a counterclaim or an affirmative defense, and which defendant has the more substantial defense.

2.13 How Long is Enough?

The opening statement should be long enough to explain what needs to be explained, yet short enough to maintain the attention of the fact finders. Some opening statements may only last a few minutes, others will extend for an hour or more. There is no optimum length for an opening statement because each opening depends upon the evidence and circumstances of the case, the speaking ability of the attorney and the attention span of the fact finder. Limits may be placed on the length of an opening. An attorney who anticipates that the opposing lawyer may exceed reasonable time limits may ask that a limit be imposed.

2.14 Should You Wait to Open?

An opening statement should never be waived because of the advantages an effective opening statement provides. Perhaps an opening statement could be waived for tactical reasons if an attorney has had an opportunity to fully explain the case to the fact finder prior to the presentation of evidence. For example, in court trials, arbitrations, and administrative hearings where the fact finder becomes thoroughly familiar with the case the opening may be succinct.

Most forums permit the defendant to present an opening statement immediately after the plaintiff/prosecutor or to reserve the opening statement until immediately before the defense case begins. Applicable rules or practice may prohibit or restrict the defense option of delaying the giving of an opening. In the vast majority of civil cases and in most criminal cases, the defendant should give the opening statement immediately following the opening by the plaintiff/prosecutor. This approach provides the fact finder with an explanation of both sides of the case, places the plaintiff/prosecutor's case in perspective, and counters an effective opening statement. When the defense opening is delayed, the fact finder may attach undue weight to the initial opening statement and not fully consider available defenses.

In civil cases, because of discovery, preliminary conferences, and settlement negotiation efforts, the defense knows what issues the plaintiff will attempt to prove and what evidence will be introduced. In these cases, the advantages in immediately giving the opening usually far outweigh any advantage gained from delaying the opening.

In criminal cases, there may be an advantage to the defendant in reserving an opening statement, especially where the prosecutor has had limited discovery and does not know what the defense will be. Reserving the opening statement in such situations prevents the prosecution from modifying the presentation of its case to reduce the impact of the anticipated defense. Also, in a case where alternative defenses exist and a defense attorney is unsure what defense to use, it may be more effective to make that decision after the prosecution has presented its evidence. In some cases where the defense attorney is not certain whether the defendant will testify, delaying the opening may also be a useful tactic. Not giving an opening, however, may create an impression that the prosecution's case is stronger than it is.

2.15 Write It Out

The material for an opening statement should be organized into an outline format. The outline should include the introduction, the body, and the conclusion. The use of an outline helps organize the facts and theories of the case into a readily accessible format. As the attorney prepares other aspects of the case, this outline may be modified or altered and should remain flexible.

Some attorneys find it advantageous to prepare a complete written opening statement. This draft may then be reviewed and improved. With this format, the attorney knows that the final script of the opening statement will contain everything that needs to be presented. The drawback of using a script during an opening statement is the temptation to read it. A better approach for the attorney is to prepare a key word outline. After becoming completely familiar with the material, the attorney should be able to present the opening statement using only the key word outline.

2.16 Rehearse

Openings need to be practiced until the advocate can effectively present the opening. The attorney should practice silently and out loud, concentrating initially on content. As the content of the opening statement is mastered, the attorney can work on stylistic improvements. After this preparation the attorney should continue rehearsing the opening statement. The attorney may use an audience of colleagues, family, a mirror, or videotape for review and critique.

The attorney should rehearse until the story can be told in a persuasive, compelling manner. The attorney should not necessarily try to memorize or remember exact words used during the practice sessions, but rather express the ideas that have been rehearsed in these sessions. The key to an effective presentation of an opening statement is that the attorney knows the ideas and important phrases that need to be conveyed, is comfortable with this story, and can make a sincere, believable, and understandable presentation.

C. HOW TO ORGANIZE

2.17 Use a Structure

Opening statements must be presented in a structured fashion. While there are many possibilities that may be effective the structure should allow the entire case to be framed in the opening and should be clear, simple and straightforward and help the fact finder understand the facts and theories easily. The following are examples of various structures:

2.17.1 Time

A chronological description of events is relatively easy to remember, makes sense, and is easy to understand. The attorney describes the events in the order in which they occurred. For example, in an employment law case, the opening can begin when the plaintiff was hired and conclude with the events occurring on the date the plaintiff was fired.

2.17.2 Flashback

The beginning of the opening can explain the end of the story, and the remaining story can be told by flashing back to earlier events. For example, in a murder case, the murder can be described first, followed by the events leading up to the murder, including the preparation and planning.

2.17.3 Parallel Events

The actions of the plaintiff and the defendant or victim and criminal defendant can be told separately with the conclusion being the final event at which they came together. For example, in an automobile accident case, the routes of the plaintiff and defendant can be described with the conclusion being the collision.

2.17.4 Claims, Defenses, Topics

The opening can be structured around the claims, defenses or related topics that will be proved during the trial. For example, in a breach of commercial contract arbitration, the opening can describe the elements: creation of a contract, its breach, and the resulting damages.

2.17.5 Order of Evidence

The opening can be structured to reflect the order in which the evidence is presented, the witnesses testify, and the documents are introduced. For example, in an administrative law case involving lay and expert witnesses and numerous documents, the opening statement can follow the order in which the witnesses will testify and documents will be introduced.

2.17.6 Liability and Damages

In civil cases, the opening can first discuss liability and then damages. For example, in a personal injury case, the story can describe how the accident happened and then what injuries the plaintiff suffered.

2.17.7 Mixture of Substructures

A number of these approaches can be used for parts of the opening, as substructures. For example, a civil case could begin with the flashback technique, use chronology to present the liability facts, and explain the damages in the order in which the witnesses will describe the damages.

2.18 Parts of the Opening Statement

An opening statement has at least three major parts: the introduction, the body, and the closing.

2.19 The Introduction

The beginning of the opening needs to be carefully planned to take full advantage of the fact finder's initial attention. Starting the statement in an interesting and dramatic way may be the most effective way to begin an opening. Beginning remarks in an opening statement need to take into account what has occurred previously in a case.

Example (Judge in a Jury Trial)

Members of the Jury, at this beginning stage of the trial the attorneys will now make what is called an opening statement. Each of them will tell you the evidence that will be introduced in this case. After these opening remarks, each of the parties will present their case. The plaintiff will proceed first, and present her witnesses and introduce documents which support her case. Defense counsel will then have an opportunity to cross-examine the plaintiff's witnesses. After the plaintiff introduces all her evidence, the defendant will then present witnesses and exhibits, and the plaintiff will have a chance to question the defense witnesses. After both parties have completed presenting their evidence, the attorneys will have an opportunity to summarize and explain the case to you in final argument. I will then instruct you on the law by explaining the law that applies to this case. You will then go to the jury room, deliberate and reach a verdict which will conclude this trial.

Counsel for plaintiff will now make the initial opening statement.

Ordinarily a judge provides a similar or even more concise explanation to the jury describing how the trial will be conducted. If the attorney is uncertain whether the judge will give any instructions, the attorney can request that the judge provide particular instructions and preliminary remarks. If a judge does not explain to the jury the trial procedures, the attorney may provide that information at some point during the opening statement.

2.20 Explanation of Purposes

An opening statement may begin with an explanation of who the attorneys are, who they represent, and the purposes of an opening statement. These remarks may be unnecessary in a court trial, arbitration and administrative hearing. The advantage of these or similar preliminary remarks is that the fact finder may better understand the purpose of the opening statement and the identity of the attorneys and parties. The disadvantage of such remarks is that they may not be the most persuasive way to begin the presentation of the case. The following examples of introductory comments demonstrate how some lawyers begin their opening in jury trials.

Example (Purpose)

Members of the Jury, this opening statement allows me to explain to you the evidence that you will hear and see in this case. The evidence will be presented in bits and pieces and not in the order in which the events happened. This opening will provide you with an overview of the case and help you understand what happened.

Example (Explanation)

My name is Atticus Finch. I represent Tom Robinson, who is sitting here. I now have the privilege of speaking to you about the evidence that will be introduced during this trial. This case will be presented to you like a jigsaw puzzle. Each witness who testifies and each document that is admitted will be a piece of that puzzle. At the end you will be able to put that picture together by yourselves. In the beginning, this opening statement allows me an opportunity to describe to you each of the pieces so that you will be better able to understand the complete picture.

Example (Personal Injury)

Ms. Duncan, the plaintiff, has suffered severe and permanent injuries caused by the negligent driving of the defendant, Mr. Bugatti. As you know, I am Max Steuer, the attorney representing Ms. Duncan. As the judge explained, this opening statement permits me to talk with you about what happened to cause that accident and to cause those disabling injuries. I will tell you the story of what happened and a summary of what the witnesses will describe.

Example (Employment Contract Case)

You have already met the plaintiff, Ms. Parker. She is in court today to be paid the salary the defendant promised to pay her. I am here today to present the facts through witnesses and documents which show that she is entitled to that money. You are here today to listen to that evidence and award her the money owed her.

2.21 Explanation of Theme

An opening statement may begin with an explanation of the case theory described in a compelling and dramatic way to develop interest. The advantage of this approach is that the fact finder gains a favorable impression of the case and is more likely to recall the theme words used to describe the important facts and issues. The disadvantage of such an approach is that issues may be overstated, or the opening too melodramatic.

Example (Personal Injury)

This case is about the life and death of a man, a husband, a father, and a productive member of this community. His name was Ward Nelson. He was killed when the jeep he was driving rolled over, throwing him out of the jeep and over the cliff where he fell to his death. He was thirty-one years old with a family, a wife, two boys, and a full life ahead of him.

Example (Product Liability Plaintiff)

You are going to hear a case of corporate deception and the greed by one of the largest pharmaceutical manufacturers in the world. The case is about the marketing of a product, the Precon Shield, an untested and unsafe product. The case is about the selling of this product to thousands of women without caring about the serious injuries these women suffered because of this dangerous and defective product.

Example (Criminal Prosecution)

On a clear summer evening on July 15, Della Southern got off the commuter train in Elmhurst. She was coming from work in downtown Mitchell where she works as a legal assistant. The train pulled away from the station. She crossed the tracks and began walking towards her car parked a block from the train station in a parking ramp. As she walked into the entrance of the parking ramp, she heard a noise. She turned to her right and confronted that man (looking at the defendant). On behalf of the people of this state, I am here today to tell you the facts of what happened when she confronted that man (pointing to the defendant). After hearing those facts, it will be clear beyond a reasonable doubt that that man (turning to the defendant) brutally assaulted Ms. Southern and stole her purse, her money, and her sense of security and peace of mind.

Example (Criminal Defense)

This is a case of mistaken identity. Mr. Ramirez did not commit any crime on the evening of July 15. He is innocent of what the prosecutor has claimed he did. Under our system of justice, the prosecution has the burden to prove to you beyond a reasonable doubt that my client is guilty. Under our system of justice, Mr. Ramirez is presumed to be innocent. Indeed he is innocent as he sits here in this courtroom. The facts that you will hear in this case will convince you that there is more than a reasonable doubt that my client was anywhere near the scene of the crime. The case for the prosecution consists of one eyewitness who attempts to identify my client. That identification was made under circumstances which make it totally unreliable.

2.22 The Body

The advocate should design a presentation to explain each fact and element of the case in understandable terms. The lawyer's knowledge of the case will be extensive and may cause obvious facts to go unmentioned during the opening. The attorney must keep in mind the fact finder will be hearing the full case for the first time.

An opening statement must answer at least six simple questions: Who is involved? What happened? Where? When? How did it happen? Why did it happen? The most effective way this information can be presented is usually by the attorney telling a compelling and complete story. The story should parallel the substance of the evidence, and the summary that will be given in the closing argument. An advocate, particularly a defense counsel, may need to explain what the evidence will not show as well as what the evidence will show.

2.23 The Conclusion

An opening statement should have a strong conclusion. This may be achieved with a concise summary of the vital facts, with a compelling statement justifying a decision, or with a dramatic summary of the major theme of the case. A strong presentation can be hindered by an apologetic or weak conclusion. The final words should be well thought out, so that no matter how lost the attorney gets, the conclusion will be effective both in words and delivery.

Example (Civil Plaintiff)

Based on all the evidence we will prove to you that the defendant is responsible for the injuries suffered by Ms. Didrickson and that you find that the defendant must compensate her for her medical expenses, for the wages and income that she lost, and for the pain and suffering she has suffered as a result of the defendant's negligence on the golf course that day.

Example (Civil Defendant)

Those facts clearly establish the defendant was not liable and has no responsibility to the plaintiff in this case. At the end of this case, based on this evidence, you will conclude the defendant did no wrong and bears no responsibility. We will ask you then to issue an award on his behalf, a decision in support of Edmund Fitzgerald against the claimant.

Example (Criminal Prosecution)

At the conclusion of this trial, I will have an opportunity to talk with you again. I will discuss some of the things I've said today and the evidence you will hear in the trial. I will ask you at that time to return a just and fair verdict and find the defendant guilty of robbery.

Example (Criminal Defendant)

At the end of this case, I will discuss what you have heard and seen during the trial. By that time, you will have more than reasonable doubt that B. Baggins was involved in the incident. By that time, you will be convinced that Mr. Baggins did not steal the ring and is not guilty. By that time you will know he is innocent, and that you must conclude he is not guilty.

2.24 Opening Statement Critique

Questions that may assist in determining whether an opening statement has been properly constructed include the following:

Does the opening statement tell what happened?

Does the opening statement tell the fact finder why to find for the client?

Does the opening statement make the fact finder want to find for the client?

Does the opening statement tell how to find for the client?

Does the opening statement have a structure that is clear and simple?

Is the opening statement consistent with what will be proved and with what will be argued in summation?

Does the opening make the fact finder weep (not for you, but for your client)?

D. TELL A STORY

The exact content of an opening depends upon the facts and circumstances of the case and the strategic and tactical decisions of the attorney. The following factors should be considered when preparing the opening statement.

2.25 An Effective Story

The opening statement story should be told with simple language, in as dramatic a fashion as is appropriate, and in an interesting way. Things that make a story very interesting and very believable appear in great works of literature, art, and theatre, and they are the same things that make an opening statement very effective.

Example (Commercial Case)

This is a story of a lost business opportunity, a lost invention, a lost dream—lost by an inexperienced individual to a large and sophisticated corporation. On February 14, Dr. Kirbuck, while working hard and long hours, by herself and for herself, in her home workshop, invented a new and innovative electronic computer device. Sometime later she visited the offices of the defendant. She offered the defendant an opportunity to buy this invention. The lawyers for that corporation drafted an 18–page, single-spaced contract. The executives of that corporation told the plaintiff that if she wanted to market her invention she would need to sign this contract. She signed it. They signed it. She lived up to her end of the bargain. They have not lived up to their end of the contract. They breached the terms of that contract. They did not do what they told her they would do. They have not paid her what they told her they would pay her. We are here today to hold them to their promise, to their word, to the written contract.

Example (Negligence)

On the evening of July 20, Jamie Summers was just finishing the last half mile of her three mile run down Highway 100 here in Culver City. Mr. Bung had just finished drinking his fourth or fifth martini at the Mermaid bar. As Jamie was running about four miles an hour on the marked jogging path along Highway 100, Bung was weaving his car from side to side about 60 miles per hour along southbound Highway 100. Jamie never saw the car that ran her over. Jamie never saw the driver that killed her. She is gone. Her life is over. But we can see him, he is with us. He sits in that chair over there. This trial is to hold Mr. Bung responsible for the reckless killing and negligent homicide of Jamie Summers—a tragedy that should never have happened.

2.26 Details

The facts presented during an opening statement should be as detailed as necessary to provide a clear and complete story. The advantage of providing a detailed story is that the story is usually perceived as more credible and more persuasive. Detail that provides necessary information for a full understanding and explains sources of corroboration or credibility usually bolsters the essential aspects of a case. The disadvantage of detailing specific facts is that the subsequent presentation of that evidence may not be as specific as the opening statement suggested. Further, too much detail can be boring and unpersuasive.

Example (Personal Injury)

In this case defendants violated school district safety rules regarding gym activities. These rules require gym mats to contain two and a half inches of thick foam. The defendants were using two inch thick pads. The school district rules require one supervisor for every ten kids using the gym mats. The defendants had only one supervisor for twenty kids.

Example (Technical Data)

We will hear a lot of technical data about this machine. We will see instruction manuals, diagrams, blueprints, and other documents. And although these engineering details may appear very complicated and technical, the basic issue in this case is simple and understandable. We will be focusing on one part of the machine which was properly designed, was safely used, and did not cause the accident.

2.27 Parties/Witnesses

Information about the parties and witnesses can be explained during opening. Witnesses should be described in a way that will make their story understandable and their testimony credible.

The fact finder needs to understand that a case involves people and not merely abstract legal problems. The more a party and key witnesses are personalized and described as individuals who will testify to what happened, the more likely the fact finder will accept them and find them believable. Statements should be made which help the fact finder identify, relate to, and empathize with the witnesses.

Whether every witness needs to be identified during opening statement depends on the facts of the case and the importance of the witness to the case. The more critical the individual is to the case, the more essential it is to identify that individual. If the testimony of the witness should be highlighted, identifying the witness in the opening statement will help to do so. If a distinguished expert will testify, identifying that expert will help.

The fact finder may have a difficult time identifying with witnesses who are not described during an opening. Fact finders will have no way of forming a picture in their mind of the witness. A party or witness who is present can be identified. Key witnesses may be present during the opening so the attorney can introduce them. The names and identities of the witnesses can also be written on a visual aid.

Statements about the background of a witness may also be included. This information can be effective if the fact finder has things in common with the background of the witness or if the description portrays the witness as a responsible individual who can be believed. The backgrounds of minor or problem witnesses need not be detailed in the opening statement.

Describing a witness during the opening commits the attorney to calling that witness to testify. Only witnesses who are sure to be called ought to be described. If there is uncertainty about whether a witness will testify, no specific reference ought to be made to that witness.

Whatever is said about a witness and testimony should be proved during the case. An attorney should not offer incomplete information or exaggerate the background or testimony of the witness. Exaggeration may create unfulfilled expectations with the fact finder. Misstatements provide an opportunity for opposing counsel to correct the inaccurate or incomplete description during opening or comment during final argument on the failure to prove such statements.

Example (Corporation)

The defendant corporation is a group of people, of individuals, who work at all levels of the company to provide services to consumers. The people of this company include workers, managers, and shareholders. Gordon Gecko, who sits here, represents all those individuals involved in the company. He will stay throughout the entire case, and he will also take the stand and testify.

Example (Witnesses)

Please consider the testimony of the witnesses carefully. Consider what they say and assess their believability. See which one has a position to protect or a reason to be less than honest. See which one was in the best position to observe what happened. We know what Mr. Jake will say in this case because we had an opportunity to ask him questions under oath before this hearing. We are sure he will tell you the same things he told us. This is what he will tell you.

Example (Experts)

Rachel Carson will testify that in her opinion this product is harmful to the environment. We will hear all about her environmental expertise, her extensive professional experiences, the many articles she has written, the teaching positions that she holds, and her reputation in her profession. We will also hear her expert opinion, the facts that support that opinion, and the reasons why that opinion is correct.

2.28 The Event

The description of the incident, occurrence, or event is a typical part of an opening statement, particularly when that occurrence is important. The description should be accurate and complete and should enable the fact finder to create a clear picture. Verbal descriptions of scenes can become complicated if too much detail is given, or if complex descriptions are made. Only those details that portray the scene accurately should be given. It can be difficult to follow directions or visualize matters in the abstract. Visual aids and exhibits may be used to describe scenes in order to ensure that the fact finder understands what is being described.

Example (Use of Diagram in Civil Case)

The streetcar was headed east, in this direction on the diagram, along Main Street. The bus stopped at this intersection here at the southwest corner of University Avenue. Main Street runs east and west, and University Avenue runs north and south along this line. The plaintiff, Stanley Kowalski, got off the streetcar at this intersection. He waited for the lights to change and waited for the walk sign, and then he began walking in the crosswalk across Main Street to the northwest side of the intersection of Main and University to this spot.

2.29 Circumstances

Information about the circumstances surrounding an incident or event may be important and may need to be explained during the opening. Explanations of the time, date, weather, equipment, and other information should be provided to the extent necessary. The more important the circumstance is to the story, the more detail should be provided. If the time of the day is critical to the case, the precise time should be mentioned. If the exact weather conditions are important, weather details should be provided.

Example (Criminal Case)

As Ms. O'Keefe walked down the first block towards her studio, she saw a number of apartment buildings on her left and to her right she saw a gas station, a grocery store, and a few homes. As she walked down the second block, she could see more apartments and more homes on both sides of the street. It was twilight. The streetlamps were on. There were three streetlamps on the second block: one in the middle and one at each end. The apartment buildings all had outside lights that were turned on. The evening sky was clear.

2.30 What Happened

The fact finder must be told what happened. The facts and circumstances of a case dictate the parameters of this part of the story. A description of what happened includes references to the parties, the scene, and circumstances. An effective description includes statements that are objectively accurate, complete, and believable. A description that is too abstract, too subjectively biased or incomplete is not persuasive.

Example (Criminal Case)

Mr. Jordan was holding the straps of the duffel bag in his right hand as he walked toward the gym. The defendant came up to him and grabbed one strap of the duffel bag and attempted to steal the bag. Mr. Jordan immediately looked right at the defendant, and instinctively gripped the handle of the duffel bag tightly. As the defendant tried to pull the bag away, Mr. Jordan again looked at the defendant and pulled the duffel bag towards himself. The defendant held onto that bag, and was pulled closer towards Mr. Jordan until the defendant's face was only about a foot away from Mr. Jordan's face.

2.31　How It Happened

Usually an issue in a case will revolve around the question of how something happened, and an explanation will be part of the opening. An explanation of the facts that describe the "how" of what happened is essential.

Example (Civil Case)

Ms. Moffetal suffered a ruptured disc in the accident. We will learn from the doctors who will testify that the spinal column is made up of a number of bones or vertebrae, one on top of the other. Between each of these bones is something called an intervertebral disc. It is shaped like a donut and acts like a shock absorber. The center of the donut is filled with something called nucleosis pulposis, a gelatin or jelly-like substance. If the vertebrae are jammed together pressure can be put on these "donuts" and the "jelly" squirts out the side (descriptive gesture). This is a rupture and the injury is called a ruptured disc. This model shows the vertebrae and discs.

Example (Civil Case/Third Party Defendant)

The evidence will show that it was Cornelius Krum who was at fault. Mr. Krum didn't oil the machine, and did not check to see if parts were worn. The machine was not faulty. Cornelius Krum ran the machine way too fast. The defendant did not cause the machine to explode, it was Mr. Krum. The defendant did not cause the plaintiff's injuries, it was Mr. Krum. The evidence will show that the defendant is not responsible for what happened, but rather Cornelius Krum was and is responsible.

2.32　Why it Happened

Explaining the what and the how of a story may not be sufficient if the why has not been explained. The why may not be of critical importance in a legal sense, but the fact finder may be curious about why something happened. If a good reason exists to explain the "why," then a concise explanation should be included in an opening. Explanations of why something happened usually are limited in an opening because a detailed or lengthy explanation may go beyond the evidence of a case and become improper argument. If an explanation cannot be based on direct or circumstantial evidence, then an explanation should be reserved for final argument.

Example (General)

Why were the defendants in a hurry? Because they were late for a skittleball game.

Example (Medical Negligence)

This is a case about medical negligence. Doctor Frank Burns was careless when he performed surgery on the plaintiff. He is not a bad doctor. He is not unfit to practice medicine. He made a serious mistake, and he must be held responsible the same way any professional must be held responsible for a serious mistake that causes pain and suffering and damages. He made the mistake, in part, because he was tired. He had been up all night working at the hospital and had not slept.

E. TELL MORE OF THE STORY

2.33 Prefatory Phrases

Attorneys may use a variety of prefatory phrases during opening statements. Some common prefaces include "I will prove" and "the evidence will show." Whether prefatory phrases should be used is a matter of debate among advocates. Some suggest that none of these phrases should be used but that the attorney should simply tell a story without any qualifying prefaces. Some advocates believe the attorney must use phrases like "I will prove to you" or "I will present evidence" to establish the attorney's position in a case and to have as powerful an influence as possible. Other trial advocates believe that more objective phrases such as "the evidence will be" or "you will learn" are the more appropriate phrases.

In proceedings where the attorneys have the flexibility to say what they want, the decision about whether a preface should be used and what the preface should state is usually a tactical decision based upon who the fact finder is and the attorney's preference. Those attorneys who feel strongly that they must state what they will prove will use such prefaces. Those attorneys who believe that telling a story is more effective will not use certain phrases because they believe that such phrases as "I will prove" unnecessarily place the attorney in the center of the opening statement and de-emphasize the facts. Some attorneys also believe that phrases, such as "the evidence will show," reduce the impact of the story and remind the audience that what is being said has yet to be proved.

The use of some phrases during an opening may prevent a presentation from sounding like an argument. A neutral qualifying introduction such as "you will learn" or "the evidence will prove" may be an effective way of preventing an objection. If this tactic is overused, however, and it becomes apparent it is being used to argue or to introduce otherwise inappropriate information, an objection will be sustained.

Example (Criminal Case)

I will prove the defendant did not intend to shoot the gun. I will present evidence to you that will establish this incident was all a tragic accident.

Example (Civil Case)

You will learn from the evidence the defendant was negligent. Because he was negligent he is responsible for what happened. The facts will prove that because the defendant is responsible he must be held accountable and must compensate the plaintiff for what he did to her.

2.34 Visual Aids and Exhibits

In addition to diagrams, visual aids and exhibits significantly increase the effectiveness of an opening statement. These devices help the fact finder understand the facts and details of the case. Visual aids that provide an outline of the issues on charts explaining complex issues can be particularly helpful in visualizing parts of a story. An attorney should use them whenever their use will make it easier for the attorney to explain and easier for the fact finder to understand something.

Visual aids may be created exclusively for use during opening statement. Exhibits that will be real or demonstrative evidence can also be used. Some jurisdictions have restrictions on the use of visual aids and exhibits. Permission for their use should be sought before the opening to avoid an interruption or objection from opposing counsel.

Example (Injuries)

You will see some photographs of the plaintiff's injuries during this trial. Some of them may be difficult to look at. But you need to see them so that you can understand the full extent of the plaintiff's injuries. They are not shown to you for their shock effect. If they do shock you somewhat, remember that they are really only a pale imitation of what the real injuries were and much less shocking than if you saw the real injuries in the flesh. I am going to show you a few now. This first one is how the plaintiff looked one day after the accident.

Example (Product Liability)

Here is a chart listing the design and manufacturing defects. We want to review each of these items with you. This first column lists the defects. This second column lists the dates when the defendant first knew about the defects, and this third column lists what injuries the defects caused. This chart will help you understand what went wrong and why it went wrong.

2.35 Claims and Defenses

References to the claims or defenses should be made.

Example (Civil Case)

The evidence will show that respondent signed this contract and failed to deliver the goods that she promised to deliver to the claimant according to the terms of this contract. The issue you will need to resolve is whether the goods that respondent did ship were the goods the claimant ordered under the agreement.

Example (Civil Case)

The primary question you will need to answer in this case is whether this piece of paper is a legally enforceable and binding contract. The evidence will show that this paper is not a contract and that respondent is not responsible to the claimant. The main issue is whether this piece of paper is a legal contract, and not whether the goods were delivered.

2.36 Disputed Issues

The fact finder will focus on the disputed issues between the parties. A reference to the conflict in the evidence or testimony helps the fact finder understand what they have to decide.

Example (General)

There will be a dispute in the evidence presented to you—a disagreement about who said what. Ms. Scarlett will say the light was red, while Mr. Teal will say the light was green. After hearing both sides, we believe you will agree that Ms. Scarlett is mistaken and Mr. Teal is correct and find that the light was green.

2.37 The Law

The attorney may make refer to the law and blend a discussion of the law with the facts.

Example (Negligence by Defendant)

You will learn that there was a stop sign at the intersection of Boardwalk and Park Place and that a person driving through that intersection must come to a complete stop and look in both directions before proceeding. The evidence will show that the defendant failed to come to a full, complete stop at the stop sign at the intersection of Boardwalk and Park Place as she was required by law to do.

Example (Lack of Negligence)

Negligence is the failure to exercise ordinary care—the failure to do something that a reasonable prudent person would have done under the same or similar circumstances. When you apply the appropriate legal standard to the facts of this case, it will be clear that the defendant did exercise ordinary care when she drove the buggy and is not responsible for the accident.

2.38 Burden of Proof

It may be appropriate to mention the burden of the proof in the opening statement if doing so is tactically advantageous.

Example (Civil Case)

This is a civil case. The burden of proof in a civil case is called "preponderance of the evidence." That means that the plaintiff wins if it is more probable than not that her story is true. We will prove that it is more likely than not that what the plaintiff said happened, actually happened. The burden of proof is not beyond a reasonable doubt, which is a much heavier burden. That applies in criminal cases, not in civil cases like this one. Judge Hand will explain this lesser burden of proof later during the trial, and we will apply it to this case to show you why the plaintiff is entitled to your verdict.

2.39 Damages in a Civil Case

In a civil case the plaintiff needs to explain the types of injuries, expenses, and other damages. In a contract case, the damages may be computed by referring to the terms of the contract or by establishing the lost income or profits. In a tort case, personal injury damages should include an explanation of the injury, diagnosis, treatment, and prognosis.

Example (Personal Injury)

This case is about what happened to Scott Lane as a person. He was one person before the accident and a different person after. Your task is to put a value on the differences between what Scott was and what he has become and will remain for the rest of his life.

Example (Pain and Suffering)

Plaintiff will tell you the horrors she went through during four months of intensive burn treatments. She will tell you that her twice daily bath was so excruciatingly painful she screamed. She will tell you that she has never experienced any pain like the pain caused from her burns. She will explain that she could not use enough drugs to eliminate the pain because the drugs made her even sicker. She will describe to you the pain with which she has to live.

2.40 Amount of Damages

Lawyers who prefer a detailed description of damages want the fact finder to know from the outset the extent of the damages sought. Mentioning a dollar amount creates a frame of reference, establishes the severity of the damages, suggests that the attorney knows what the case is worth, and preconditions the fact finder to a request in summation for a large damage award. Lawyers who prefer a minimal description of damages want the fact finder to first hear the details during the proceeding. Not mentioning the dollar amount during the opening delays the disclosure of damages to the introduction of damage evidence, creates suspense, avoids locking the attorney and witnesses into set positions, and gives the fact finder an opportunity to hear the witnesses describe the injuries before a request for specific damages is made.

If the injuries that caused the damages are slight, less emphasis should be placed on them. If the injuries that caused the damages are great, more emphasis should be placed on them during the opening.

Example (Damages Described)

This case involves the amount of responsibility that the defendant bears as a result of this tragedy. The law measures the amount of responsibility in dollars. You will hear evidence about the substantial injuries the plaintiff has suffered as a result of the accident. These damages amount to $1,256,000, which is a substantial amount of money—but an amount which is fair and reasonable because the responsibility the defendant has in this case is equally substantial.

Example (Damages Reserved)

At the conclusion of the case, we will discuss the evidence that you have heard. We will ask at the conclusion of the case that you return a verdict that will fairly and adequately compensate the plaintiff for what she has been put through. We will also ask you to return a verdict which will include punitive damages—damages which punish the defendant for gross misconduct. Punitive damages are available under the law in cases of this nature when a manufacturer recklessly makes a product. Punitive damages tell the defendants they did something wrong and shouldn't ever do it again. The defendant corporation has a net worth in excess of $100 million. At the end of the case, I will come back and request you to award the plaintiff an amount of money that will compensate her for what happened and award her additional money that will tell the defendants they were reckless.

2.41 Request for Verdict

An opening statement should contain an explanation of the decision that the facts will support. This explanation should be clear and distinct so the fact finder understands what conclusion must be reached.

Example (Civil Case)

Now I've told you what this case is all about. You will hear from the witnesses just what happened, and you will have documents that will support that testimony. At the close of all the evidence I am going to ask you to bring back a verdict in favor of the plaintiff and against the defendant in an amount to compensate her fully for her injury.

Example (Criminal Case)

The testimony and exhibits will prove that the Defendant shot and killed J.R. Ewing. The evidence will prove that the Defendant intended to shoot J.R. Ewing, intended to kill J.R. Ewing, and that the Defendant thought about it for three days beforehand. These facts will prove beyond a reasonable doubt that the defendant is guilty of first degree murder.

F. USE PERSUASIVE TECHNIQUES

The following sections involve techniques that apply to the presentation of an opening statement. These approaches need to be reviewed to determine their applicability to an opening statement in a particular case.

2.42 Offensive/Defensive Approaches

An opening statement should lead the fact finder to a conclusion that a party is entitled to win. The plaintiff will naturally take the "offensive" and explain the story in a positive way. Some defense counsel may think it appropriate for the opening statement to be explained in a "defensive" way because the plaintiff has the burden of proof. A more effective tactic may be for the defense to take the offensive and explain what the defendant's evidence will prove and then defend the case by stating what the plaintiff's evidence will not prove.

Counsel for the defendant who presents an opening after the opening by the plaintiff must decide whether and how to respond to the opening by the opposing attorney. The opening by defendant should describe the case of the defendant and, after that has been explained, respond to the extent necessary to statements by the plaintiff in the initial opening statement. Even in a criminal case where the defendant will not testify, the opening statement for the defense should be as positive as possible. The defense will present evidence through cross-examination of the prosecution's witnesses, and this information can be used to support reasonable doubt.

At the end of the opening statement for the plaintiff, counsel for the plaintiff may raise some questions or make some remarks which the attorney suggests defense counsel should respond to or address during the opening for the defendants. Counsel for the defendant should present the prepared opening statement and should avoid directly responding to plaintiff's tactic, unless a response is necessary or would be more effective than not responding.

Example (Civil Case)

At the end of her opening statement, counsel for the plaintiff suggested to you that I should tell you what facts we had which differed from the facts she explained to you. You may have wondered why I did not respond to the questions she raised until now. The facts that I just explained to you that you will hear from the witnesses who take that stand and which you will read in these documents will answer those questions.

2.43 Anticipating Defenses

After making an opening statement, the plaintiff has no opportunity for rebuttal after the defense opening. The plaintiff should anticipate defenses and deal with them in the opening. In civil cases, the plaintiff will usually know the defenses the defendant will raise and attempt to explain away such defenses.

In criminal cases, the constitutional rights of the defendant limit comments that can be made by the prosecution. The prosecutor may not directly comment on evidence the defense may produce. A prosecutor can explain evidence that will be introduced during the prosecutor's case and state indirectly that such evidence overcomes potential defenses, but the prosecution cannot comment on possible testimony by the defendant because the defendant need not and may not testify or present any witnesses.

Example (Accident Case)

The defendant will try to avoid responsibility in this case by telling you the accident was Alice's own fault—that she wasn't watching where she was walking. But after hearing all the evidence, you will learn this was an area that people walked all the time and no one—including Alice—would expect there to be a hole in the ground.

Example (Automobile Case)

Now I must tell you that the defendant will try to put some of the blame for this accident on James Dean. The defendant will claim that Mr. Dean should have stopped his car or swerved to avoid the accident. But you will learn the defendant came into that blind intersection so fast there was no way Mr. Dean could have avoided the collision—he just could not see or avoid the defendant's car.

2.44 Asserting Promises

A "promise" that certain evidence will prove a certain fact can be effective as long as the attorney can fulfill that promise. A promise that is not kept causes the fact finder to lose confidence in the attorney. A promise is a tactical approach that must be employed carefully. If a lawyer does make promises during an opening or otherwise asserts that certain evidence will be proved, the opposing lawyer should note all these statements and mention during summation all promises not kept.

Example (General)

I promise you that I will present evidence showing the defendant lied to the plaintiff about the value of this land. After hearing this evidence, you will conclude that the defendant misrepresented the facts and defrauded the plaintiff. At the end of this case, I will ask you to put us to the decisive test: Did we prove to you what we said we would prove? If we have, we will ask you then for a decision in favor of the plaintiff against the defendant.

2.45 Making a Compact

The attorney may make a covenant during the opening. The attorney may promise that the attorney will not misstate any evidence or exaggerate the facts. This tactic ought to be reserved for those situations where there is a reasonable concern the opposing lawyer will present an unfair and improper opening statement.

Example (General)

Everything that I have told you in this opening about the evidence is what you will hear from this witness stand and see and read in this contract. I will prove that the events in this case happened the way I described the facts. I ask you to hold the other parties to this same standard.

2.46 Employing Understatement

Understatement can be a useful credibility-building device for an opening statement presentation. Understating a case sets the expectation of the fact finder at a level that will be exceeded during the case. The presentation of the evidence will then surpass the fact finder's expectations, enhancing the credibility of the case and the attorney. Understatement may also arouse the fact finder's curiosity. The use of understatement does have disadvantages. It may reduce the attorney's ability to explain the facts in a persuasive way, and a fact finder may initially perceive an understated case to be weaker than the attorney intended.

Example (Civil Case)

Judy and Doralee talked that day about Violet and her future with the group. They will take the witness stand and tell you what they said. When you hear what they said, you will understand the plans they had for Violet.

2.47 Avoiding Overstatement

The attorney should avoid the use of overstatement during an opening statement. Opposing counsel may comment during closing argument about the absence of the exaggerated evidence from the case.

2.48 Asserting Difficult Positions

The facts and issues in some cases will be more difficult for the fact finder to accept than in other cases. Usually, it is easier to prove that a person was negligent, failed to do something, or made a mistake rather than having to prove that a person intentionally did something, acted very unreasonably, or lied. For example, in a negligence case where contradictory statements were made by the plaintiff and defendant regarding the color of a traffic light, the plaintiff can win by proving that the defendant could not accurately see the color of the light or was confused about the color of the light without proving the defendant is a liar. In some cases the difficult and uncomfortable position is necessary as part of the proof and these difficult facts must be addressed in the opening statement. For example, a discrimination case requires the plaintiff to prove the defendant committed a discriminatory act. In the opening statement, the attorney needs to tell the jurors exactly what will be proved.

Example (Civil Case)

We will prove to you that the defendant stated that blacks were lazy and that he didn't want them working for him, and if it seems it is not now appropriate for me to call the defendant a racist, by the end of the case it will be clear to you that he is a racist.

Example (Criminal Case)

I will prove to you that the witness for the prosecution is a liar. Joe Isuzu, whom the prosecutor has described as the key witness in this case, has lied a number of times in the past regarding what he did on the night of February 15th. He lied to the police when they questioned him. And he took an oath to tell the truth and lied to a judge at a court hearing.

2.49 Describing Case Weaknesses

Attorneys must consider whether to describe weaknesses in their own case. Weaknesses that will be brought out in testimony may need to be presented in a candid and forthright manner. Weaknesses in a case that have not been explained to the fact finder and that most likely will be mentioned during the opposition's opening statement or later in the case may need to be addressed during opening statement. An open and candid disclosure of such information may increase the appearance of sincerity and credibility of the attorney while reducing the impact of the opposition's strong points. On the other hand, an unnecessary explanation of a weakness may over-emphasize it or give it more credibility than it deserves.

Example (Negligence)

A moment ago, I told you that I would describe everything important that happened. You will learn that Mickey Morissey had stopped at a local bar on his way home from work. Mr. Morissey will tell you himself that he had dinner and two or three glasses of wine with dinner a couple of hours before the accident. The evidence will show, however, that that had nothing to do with the accident, which happened only because the defendant's car crossed over the center line.

Example (Contract)

We told you that we would put everything before you, the good and the bad. You will learn in this case that Bonnie Parker has a criminal record—she was convicted of income tax evasion over five years ago. But that has nothing to do with the fact that she had an employment contract with the defendant and that she has a contract right to her salary.

Example (Personal Injury)

In the interest of fairness, and holding nothing back, you will hear evidence from J.J. Gittes that he was a trespasser—he did not have permission to be on the property when he got hurt. But you will learn that the owner, the defendant, must take care not to injure people who are on her property whether they have permission to be there or not.

2.50 Explaining the Absence of Evidence

During the opening the attorney can describe what facts will not be proved, what documents will not be introduced, and what evidence will not be presented, and briefly explain why such information will not be offered during the case. Usually this explanation is appropriate where evidence does not exist or was not preserved. The fact finder may wonder why some evidence is not introduced, and this explains what will not be offered.

Example (Missing Witness)

The van was behind schedule when Ms. Rayette boarded it. She will tell you it was about five minutes late. The driver of the van will not be able to tell you how late the van was because he moved away from our city over a year ago and cannot be located despite our very best efforts to find him.

Example (Absent Evidence)

The evidence will be that Overland Motors did no testing on the Model C–11. Our expert, Dr. Necessiter, will testify that in his opinion proper testing would have shown the C–11 to be unreasonably dangerous and defective. Evidence will be before you that there was no warning.

2.51 Qualifying Remarks

In jury trials, some attorneys emphasize to the jurors that what an attorney says during opening does not constitute evidence. Other attorneys may explain that the jurors' function is to determine the facts after hearing the evidence during the trial. Comments like this usually reduce the impact of an opening statement presentation and are often unnecessary because the same statement may be contained in the judge's preliminary instructions to the jury. Occasionally counsel may want to make such comments in an attempt to reduce the effectiveness of a particularly persuasive opening statement made by an opponent and to remind the jurors that they must wait to determine the evidence as it is introduced during the trial.

Example (General)

You will hear a lot of lawyer talk in this case. You have just listened to the opening statement for the plaintiff. What we lawyers say is not evidence. The judge will tell you that you are not to decide this case based upon what we as lawyers have said but rather what the evidence will prove. You are not to rely on lawyer talk in reaching the verdict in this case. You are to rely on the testimony of the witnesses who will come before you and testify and the documents that will be read to you.

G. HOW TO DELIVER THE OPENING

The following additional factors will affect the quality of the opening presentation.

2.52 Stand

The attorney is usually more effective standing in front of the fact finder and not hidden behind a lectern or table. This is not to say that an effective opening cannot be presented using a lectern, but a lectern may unnecessarily interfere with an attorney establishing an effective presence.

In some courts, arbitrations and administrative hearings, it may be necessary for an advocate to stand behind a lectern when presenting the opening statement. In these situations, the attorney may ask permission to stand away from the lectern in order to make a more effective presentation. If the attorney must remain at a lectern, visual aids or exhibits may be used to emphasize points and to provide some opportunity for movement away from the lectern.

2.53 Move

Some movement is useful, particularly if the opening is long. Movement and stance should be orchestrated so as not to be distracting. An attorney may use movement as a transition or to provide emphasis. Movement that appears purposeless is usually distracting and should be avoided. Some forums may not allow movement; some court and hearing rooms may not permit movements. In these cases, stand still, or try to.

2.54 Close or Distant?

The attorney must maintain an appropriate distance from the fact finder. This distance should neither be so far away that personal contact is lost nor so close that the fact finder feels uncomfortable. A distance of between five and eight feet can be used as an appropriate guide, but the optimum distance varies in different circumstances.

2.55 Gesture

The attorney should use gestures that are appropriate to the content of the opening statement and that appear natural to the attorney. Gestures should be made even if the attorney stands behind the lectern. A fact finder will become bored with a talking head, which is all that is seen if the attorney stands behind a lectern without using any gestures, movement, or visual aids.

2.56 Look and Listen

One of the most effective ways to establish credibility, sincerity, and intention is to look directly at the fact finder during the opening statement. The eye contact must be varied, sufficiently long to establish a contact but not so long that it makes the fact finder uncomfortable.

2.57 Use Transitions

The opening statement is more effective if the attorney employs transitions in the presentation. Prefatory remarks, silence, a louder voice, a softer voice, visual aids, movement, and gestures are all devices which can signal a transition.

2.58 Observe the Fact Finder

The attorney must observe the fact finder's reactions during the opening statement and adjust the presentation accordingly. Some fact finders express reactions regarding the case during the opening statement. However, it can be difficult to determine accurately what people are thinking just by watching them during a presentation. Care must be taken not to overreact and not to change an approach completely because of a perceived reaction.

2.59 Prepare Notes and Outlines

When notes are used, the attorney should not pretend not to use them or try to sneak a peek. An obvious use of notes done openly can be effective. Prepared outlines can be effectively employed in an opening conducted with the use of visual aids. A prepared diagram, blackboard, whiteboard, easel paper, or an overhead transparency may contain an outline of the opening which highlights important matters and assists the attorney in explaining the facts.

H. COMPLEX CASES

2.60 Opening Statements in Complex Cases

Complex issues need to be presented in an uncomplicated way. The primary challenge is to explain to the fact finder the issues in the most simple and straightforward manner possible. The mind set of a fact finder involved in a complex case may be that the issues are complex. The task of the attorney is to present these issues so the fact finder will perceive the case to be a series of simple issues that need to be resolved.

The significance of the issues and the amount of resources available in a complex case may permit the use of some approaches that would be unavailable in simpler cases. Methods involving the use of creative and innovative visual aids will be an effective way to uncomplicate issues. Diagrams, charts, overhead transparencies, and computer generated presentations can be highly effective methods. Consultants with experience in these areas can be retained to assist the attorney in creating these visual aids.

I. WHAT YOU CANNOT DO

2.61 What is Improper?

Certain statements and comments made during an opening are objectionable. References to the following evidence and the following comments are improper:

2.61.1 Referring to Inadmissible or Unprovable Evidence

Counsel must not refer to inadmissible evidence or unprovable facts during opening statement. This prohibition extends to evidence excluded by preliminary evidentiary rulings, or likely to be excluded by the rules of evidence, as well as facts, opinions, or inferences that are not supported by evidence. The standard for determining whether an attorney may refer to specific evidence is whether the attorney has reasonable, good faith grounds to believe the evidence will be admissible. The standard to determine whether a matter can be proved is whether there is a source of available evidence to prove the matter. The opening statement is not to be used as a subterfuge to present inadmissible or nonexistent evidence or to circumvent the rules of evidence and professional responsibility.

Objection:

Counsel has referred to evidence that is neither admissible nor provable in this case. We request that the evidence be disregarded and counsel be admonished for making such references.

Response to Objection:

Explain the evidence law that supports the admissibility of the questioned evidence.

Describe the source of evidence that will support the statement made.

Advise the judge and opposing counsel before the opening that there will be a reference to potentially objectionable evidence, and seek a preliminary ruling by the judge as to its admissibility.

Blame co-counsel for thinking up the idea.

2.61.2 Explaining the Law

The attorney in bench and administrative trials and arbitrations may explain the law. The attorney in a jury trial should not explain details of the law or give instructions to the jury. While making brief references regarding the law to the jury is proper, lengthy descriptions or detailing of the law is not proper. These descriptions are only appropriate in summation.

The precise extent to which an attorney may refer to the law during an opening to the jury varies among jurisdictions and among judges. Some courts strictly limit an attorney's explanation of the law during opening statement, and some courts permit reasonable latitude to the attorneys to explain the law applicable to the facts.

Objection:

> Counsel is improperly explaining the law or jury instructions during opening statement.

Response to Objection:

> Avoid lengthy or detailed references to the law or jury instructions.
>
> Briefly mention the law or jury instructions several times during the opening, rather than describing it in one lengthy explanation.
>
> Combine a description of the facts with an explanation of the law to make these statements sound more factual in nature.
>
> Use prefatory remarks such as "The evidence will show" before explaining the law.
>
> Remind the jurors that it is the judge and not the attorneys who will explain the law to them.
>
> Explain to the judge you always wanted to be a judge and were just practicing.

2.61.3 Making Argumentative Statements

Counsel should not make argumentative statements during the opening. The opening statement is primarily an opportunity for counsel to present the evidence that will be introduced and not to argue the facts, the law, or the case.

Objection:

Counsel is arguing.

Response to Objection:

In a jury trial immediately request a bench conference to avoid being admonished by the court in front of the jury.

Explain that the reference to the facts, law, or case is proper and necessary during opening statement and is not an argument.

Avoid speaking with an argumentative tone of voice, or with over-emphatic gestures, or in a loud, aggressive manner.

Apologize to the judge and admit being a former high school debator.

2.61.4   Stating Personal Beliefs and Opinions

The attorney should not state a personal opinion or belief concerning the evidence or the case. The fact finder is to determine the case based upon the facts and the law and not upon the personal statements of counsel. Phrases such as "I personally believe" or "It is my opinion" are objectionable. The lawyer may state, "I will prove" or "I submit" because the lawyer is not stating a personal position.

Objection:

Counsel is stating a personal belief or opinion.

Response to Objection:

Rephrase the remarks and avoid interjecting personal opinions.

Use phrases such as "We will present evidence to you that will show" and "You will learn that" rather than phrases that suggest your personal beliefs.

Tell the judge that for once, you happen to be right.

2.61.5 Putting Fact Finders in the Place of the Party

Counsel may not ask fact finders to put themselves in the place of a party or witness in determining an issue. The fact finders are to base their decision on the evidence and not substitute their personal experiences or reactions for that of the evidence presented in the case.

Objection:

> Counsel is asking the fact finders to improperly put themselves in the place of a party.

Response to Objection:

> Avoid suggesting the fact put themselves in the place of a party or witness.

> Save references to the common life experiences of the fact finders until final argument.

> Use general references to real life or common sense. The fact finders will put themselves in the place of the witness or party without being asked to do so. For example, "Mr. Burns did what most people would do" and "Ms. Allen used common sense when she turned to the right."

> Tell the judge what time the party starts.

2.61.6 Speculating About the Other Side's Case

A prosecutor in a criminal case cannot suggest what the defense will prove because the defense has no obligation to prove anything. Speculation as to the other side's case in a civil matter is argumentative, does not represent what the evidence will show, and is usually improper.

Objection:

> Counsel is improperly speculating regarding what we will prove.

Response to Objection:

> Explain the statements relate to evidence the other side will introduce and are proper.
>
> Explain it is necessary to describe facts the other side will prove in order to understand all the facts of the case.
>
> Explain you were doing what any good investment banker would do.

2.61.7 Making Disparaging Remarks

Counsel may not make remarks during opening statement which disparage opposing counsel, the opposing case, the opposing party, or witnesses. Such conduct is improper, unfairly prejudicial, and unethical.

Objection:

> Counsel is making improper remarks. Counsel has said I was mendacious and I ask your Honor to admonish counsel and insist she apologize to me.

Response to Objection:

> Try to explain that the remarks are not improper.
>
> Admit a mistake and apologize.
>
> Accept an admonition from the court without argument.
>
> Explain that the term is complimentary and hope the judge doesn't have a dictionary.
>
> Acknowledge being a jerk and accept whatever happens to you.

2.61.8 Additional Prohibitions

The issues involved in specific cases may further restrict certain references made during opening statements. In a personal injury case, references to insurance are inappropriate. In a criminal case, a prosecutor cannot comment on the failure of the defendant to testify. In all cases, counsel may not refer to matters that may affect the passion or prejudice of the fact finder, such as appeals to the family circumstances of a party or references to the wealth or poverty of a party.

2.62 Making Objections

If an objection is sustained, the attorney should correct the mistake and continue with the opening. If the objection is to the content of the opening statement, then the subject ought to be avoided. If the objection is to the form of the statement, the statement can be rephrased. If the objection is overruled, the attorney should continue with the opening and may repeat or emphasize the statement, and may preface it with "As I was saying" or "Before the interruption."

Tactically, an attorney may decide not to object but rather write down what was said and use this against the opposing attorney in closing argument. Many attorneys extend a professional courtesy to one another and do not object during opening statement unless the opponent is saying or doing something that is clearly improper and damaging to the case. Most attorneys want the openings to be presented zealously and without interruptions. However, an objection may be necessary to preserve an issue for appeal.

2.63 Asking for Curative Instructions

After an objection has been sustained in a jury trial, the attorney making the objection should consider asking the judge to instruct the jurors to disregard the improper comment. This curative instruction may reduce the negative impact of the improper comment. Some jurisdictions require the curative instruction be requested to preserve an issue for appeal. A request for a curative instruction may call more attention to the improper statement, however, and ought not to be made if the disadvantage caused by highlighting the improper comment outweighs the effectiveness of the curative instruction.

2.64 Opening Statement Motions

An opposing party may bring a motion to dismiss or for a directed verdict on an issue in the case based on admissions made during opening statement. Admissions made during the opening statement can have a binding legal effect on the party. Because the opening statement is part of the record of the case, facts conceded by counsel during the opening statement may be admissions. This motion is seldom available because rarely will the opposing counsel make such adverse admissions.

A motion to dismiss or for a directed verdict may also be brought on the ground that the opposing party has failed to establish a prima facie case during the opening. Generally, the failure to mention specific evidence in the opening does not preclude subsequent introduction of the evidence at trial. As long as the pleadings and prehearing proceedings have placed matters in issue, the rules of evidence and not the scope of the opening statement determines what evidence will be admissible and inadmissible.

In a civil trial, the judge has the discretion to grant a summary disposition based upon the opening statement of counsel. If an opening statement contains admissions or fails to refer to sufficient supporting evidence, there may be grounds for a motion to dismiss, a summary judgment, or directed verdict. In criminal cases, a judge may direct a verdict for the defendant on the basis of the prosecutor's opening statement if no reasonable juror could convict the defendant based upon the facts stated in the opening statement. Since the rules of evidence are more relaxed in arbitrations and administrative hearings the granting of a summary disposition is very unlikely.

The purpose for a summary disposition based upon the opening statement is economy. A proceeding is unnecessary if, based on the opening statement, it is obvious that no claim, defense, or case exists. Opening statements usually contain more than enough information to support a claim or defense. If a case is so weak that no facts exist to support a claim or defense, the weakness will be apparent earlier and the case should be dismissed or settled at that time. If such a summary disposition motion is granted, and evidence exists which was not described in the opening, the losing side should move to reopen the case and supplement the opening statement.

Other possible motions include:

> A motion to have the judge or arbitrator set restraints on the opponent's opening regarding time, scope, detail, and demeanor. If an attorney exceeds the reasonable standards for an opening, this motion may be granted.

> A motion by plaintiff to present additional facts in rebuttal to defendant's opening. This unusual motion may be appropriate in a situation in which the defendant raises unanticipated issues.

> A motion to change venue for an opening on Broadway.

*

RESOURCES

Bibliography

Advocacy in Opening Statements, Weyman I. Lundquist, 8 *Litigation* 23 (1982).

A Checklist for Opening Statements, Rikki J. Klieman, 8 *Trial Diplomacy Journal* 34 (1985).

Motivating Jurors Through Opening Statements, William A. Trine, 18 *Trial* 80–85 (1982).

The Opening Moment, Steven Lubet, 34 *South Texas L. R.* 109–147 (1993).

Opening Statements (Advocacy Defense of the Citizen Accused of Crime), Robert B. Hirschhorn, 43 *Mercer L. R.* 605–617 (1992).

Opening Statements, Alfred S. Julien (Callaghan 1980).

Persuasion at Trial: Opening Statements, Jeffrey T. Frederick, 33 *For the Defense* 27–29 (1991).

Storytelling in Opening Statements: Framing the Argumentation of the Trial, Kathryn Holmes Snedaker, 10 *American Journal of Trial Advocacy* 15–45 (1986).

Video

Opening Statement: Civil and Criminal, National Institute For Trial Advocacy (1977–1980).

Opening Statement in a Criminal Case, National Institute For Trial Advocacy (1977–1980).

Opening Statement: Criminal and Complex Civil Case, National Institute For Trial Advocacy (1977–1980).

Opening Statements, National Institute For Trial Advocacy (1983).

Opening Statements, Trial Practice, Anderson Publishing (1990).

Opening Statements: A Modern Approach, National Institute For
Trial Advocacy (1993).

Opening Statements in a Contract Action, Part One, National
Institute For Trial Advocacy (1987).

Opening Statements in a Contract Action, Part Two, National
Institute For Trial Advocacy (1987).

Opening Statements in a Products Liability Case, Part One, National
Institute For Trial Advocacy (1987).

Opening Statements in a Products Liability Case, Part Two,
National Institute For Trial Advocacy (1987).

Persuading the Jury in a Civil Case: Opening Statements for the
Defendants, National Institute For Trial Advocacy (1988).

Persuading the Jury in a Civil Case: Opening Statements for the
Plaintiff, National Institute For Trial Advocacy (1988).

Persuading the Jury in a Criminal Case: Opening Statements for the
Defendants, National Institute For Trial Advocacy (1988).

Persuading the Jury in a Criminal Case: Opening Statements for the
Plaintiff, National Institute For Trial Advocacy (1988).

Film

Philadelpha (1993).

Class Action (1991).

Music Box (1989).

The Verdict (1982).

To Kill a Mockingbird (1962).

Inherit the Wind (1960).

Adam's Rib (1949).

CHAPTER 3
SUMMATION

If well thou hast begun, go on; it is the end
that crowns us, not the fight.

— Robert Herrick

A. SCOPE

3.01 Be an Advocate

Summation is the final opportunity the advocate has to make an oral presentation to the fact finder. Summation usually occurs after the close of all the evidence. Summation is also known as closing argument or final argument, although the term "argument" may misstate the primary purpose of summation. It is not enough to just "argue" the rightness or wrongness of positions to the fact finder. The advocate must actually "advocate" and present a reasonable, persuasive explanation. Summation, however, can never be a substitute for the facts and the law.

3.02 What is the Purpose?

The purposes of summation are:

To summarize the factual theories and evidence of a case.

To explain persuasively the significance of the evidence presented.

To draw reasonable inferences, argue conclusions, comment on credibility, refer to common sense, and explain implications which the fact finder may not perceive.

To explain the legal theories, elements of the claims and defenses, instructions, and the law.

To highlight the rational and emotional dimensions of the case.

To answer questions from a judge or arbitrator.

To integrate the theories, evidence, and law into a cohesive and comprehensive presentation.

3.03 What is the Summation Story to be Told?

A case begins with the story told during opening statement and concludes with a story summarized during closing argument. An effective summation provides reasonable explanations, appropriately evokes the emotions of the events that occurred, and motivates the fact finders to return a favorable decision. All cases involve reasons and emotions and have facts that support the telling of a compelling story. Criminal cases involve matters of freedom and liberty. Personal injury cases involve pain and suffering. Employment cases involve the economic livelihood of people. The advocate must bring to life the emotions and feelings underlying the drama of those events.

Judges, arbitrators, administrative judges, and jurors base their decisions not only on the logic and reasons supporting a position but also on the human dimensions of the case. An intellectual argument that reaches only their minds is usually not sufficient. The advocate must present an argument that reasonably involves their emotions as well as their intellects.

The advocate must consider using these psychological and emotional influences. Every advocate has this ability. Every person has told a story to someone that touched the listener and produced appropriate feelings. This same ability will be needed during summation when the advocate must tell part of the story in a way that similarly touches the fact finders and favorably influences their judgment.

This goal of presenting a logical, reasonable, and emotional story is the art of presenting a compelling closing argument. An advocate has goals that are similar to the goals of speakers in other professions. Take a moment and think about effective speakers and consider their approaches. They not only presented information and advanced logical, reasonable positions but also said something that appropriately tapped emotions that affected decisions.

A closing argument should contain a proper balance of appeals to reason and appeals to emotion, depending upon the facts and circumstances of each case. An improper or inappropriate appeal to emotions must be avoided. An inappropriate appeal to emotions may suggest that the facts, the law, and reason do not support the advocate's position.

B. WHAT CAN BE PRESENTED

3.04 Facts and Opinions

All facts and opinions which are a part of the case, even those in dispute, may be described during summation. The advocate should discuss all important evidence and selectively discuss remaining evidence.

3.05 Inferences

Inferences are conclusions drawn from the evidence presented. Generally, the advocate may make and explain all reasonable inferences from the evidence so long as the inferences are related to the evidence presented.

3.06 The Story

The case story should be summarized in the words and phrases used throughout the case. The closing argument presents an opportunity for the advocate to connect the themes of the case with the evidence and applicable law.

3.07 The Law and the Legal Theories

During final argument, the advocate may explain how the law applies to the facts to support the result sought and how the evidence supports the legal theories.

3.08 Anecdotal References

The advocate has the opportunity during summation to use anecdotes, analogies, and metaphors involving common life experiences and to employ a variety of persuasive techniques, including the appropriate use of historical stories and appropriate references from other works of literature.

3.09 Urging a Result

The closing argument is the last opportunity the advocate has to explain and ask for a specific result.

3.10 What Not to Present

The advocate is not required to summarize or comment upon all the facts, opinions, inferences, and law involved in a case. A decision not to address an issue, an opponent's theory, or a particular fact should be based on an analysis of the importance of that subject and the ability of the advocate and the opponent to explain persuasively the position to the fact finder.

C. HOW TO PREPARE

3.11 Do It Early and Often

The planning of a case begins with the preparation of the closing argument. The factual summary and legal theories of a case that were selected in the beginning provide a framework of ideas for the closing argument. These concepts will need to be refined and revised depending on how the evidence develops during the case.

3.12 Rely on Jury Instructions

In jury trials, the judge informs the attorneys of the exact instructions of law to be provided to the jury. In many jurisdictions, the charge to the jury takes place after summation. In other jurisdictions, the judge charges the jury before summation. The attorney must review these final instructions and make certain the evidence explained in the final argument supports the law which will be explained by the judge.

All statements of law made by the attorney must be accurate. The judge will tell the jury if the attorney has explained the law differently than the judge, the jury must ignore the attorney's statement. If the attorney misstates the law, the attorney loses credibility and diminishes the impact of summation. If the attorney states the law correctly, even using the same words as the judge, the result can raise the credibility of the attorney and positively reinforce the attorney's summation.

3.13 Identify Central, Pivotal Issues

The advocate must simplify the issues. A review of the factual summaries and legal theories will determine which facts and what legal elements are undisputed and which important, controversial issues remain disputed. Evidence that has been stipulated, or uncontradicted or unrebutted, may resolve some issues.

3.14 Anticipate the Opponent's Position

The preparation of the case requires an advocate to anticipate the various theories and positions of the opposing case. By the close of the evidence, an advocate should know what the opponent will argue in summation. The advocate needs to predict the most persuasive and compelling argument that the opponent could present and analyze how to counter this argument. The more accurate the prediction, the better the chances that a final argument can be constructed to rebut or reduce the impact of the opposing argument.

3.15 Select Exhibits and Visual Aids

The advocate must decide which exhibits and visual aids are to be used during summation. Any exhibit that has been introduced during the case may be used during closing argument. Visual aids may also be created that highlight summation. These visual aids may include: a prepared chart; a summary of evidence or argument on a poster, a board, or overhead transparency; handwritten notes by the attorney on a blackboard or easel page; or an enlarged copy of the verdict form in a jury trial.

3.16 How Long is Enough?

Summation should be long enough to cover the essential arguments of the case, yet short enough to maintain the attention of the decision maker. The reasonable, optimum length for a closing argument varies depending upon the circumstances and complexity of the case and the speaking ability of the advocate. An argument that is longer than the time spent answering a law school exam is automatically unreasonable. In those jurisdictions that permit rebuttal, the advocate may need to reserve time for rebuttal. Some jurisdictions by statute or rules, and some tribunals by local practice, impose specific time limits on arguments.

3.17 Who Closes When?

The general rule is that the party who has the burden of proof closes last. Because the plaintiff/prosecutor has such a burden, the plaintiff/prosecutor usually argues last. In those jurisdictions which permit rebuttal argument, there are three summations: the plaintiff's argument, the defendant's argument, and the rebuttal argument by the plaintiff. In those jurisdictions that do not permit rebuttal, there are two summations: the defense argues first followed by the plaintiff's summation. In civil cases, in which both parties carry the burden of proof, usually the plaintiff has the opportunity to have the final argument. If the burden of proof in a civil case rests with the defendant, the defendant is permitted the last closing argument.

The advocate who argues last usually has an advantage because that advocate can rebut any argument the opponent makes. In rebuttal jurisdictions, the defense must anticipate what the plaintiff will say in rebuttal and counter those points during summation.

3.17.1 The "Opening" Summation by Plaintiff/Prosecutor

In jurisdictions that permit rebuttal, the plaintiff/prosecutor must decide what to include in the initial closing and what to save for rebuttal. In many jurisdictions the scope of rebuttal argument is limited to the points made during the defense's closing argument that were not explained during the plaintiff's initial summation. Practically, however, the scope of rebuttal is very broad because the closing argument by the opponent generally covers all important issues in the case.

3.17.2   Rebuttal Summation

Rebuttal summation should emphasize the pivotal issues not covered during the initial closing and counter points made by the defendant. A rebuttal summation is more effective if begun by advancing positive reasons, instead of beginning with defensive explanations. The points made by the defendant need to be countered during rebuttal, but rebuttal should primarily present an affirmative argument.

Rebuttal summation can be prepared in advance by predicting what the defendant will argue. This advance preparation permits the integration of the defense arguments into a restatement of the plaintiff's case theory. Any appeal to emotion should also be prepared in advance to close summation with a dramatic conclusion appropriate for the case.

3.18   Write It Out

The final argument outline that was prepared during preparation may need some revision. This final outline should include all parts of the closing argument to make certain that every matter that needs to be addressed has been included.

Some advocates prefer to write out or dictate a complete closing argument. This draft may then be reviewed and improved. This approach helps finalize the contents of the closing argument and helps determine whether some matter has been omitted. This script should not be used during the presentation of the closing argument. Reading a closing argument may be boring and significantly diminish the persuasive power of the advocate because the presentation appears dry and impersonal. To be most effective the advocate should prepare a key word outline. With practice and preparation, the outline should be all that is needed during final argument.

3.19 Rehearse

The closing argument must be rehearsed before presentation. Oral practice permits the advocate to improve both the content and the style of delivery. The advocate may rehearse the closing argument before colleagues, in front of a mirror, or on videotape for review and critique (or for sale to cable television). The advocate should practice until the summation can be presented in as persuasive a manner as possible. A thorough understanding of the argument comes through practice. When presenting the closing argument, the advocate should not necessarily attempt to recall the precise words used during the practice sessions, but express the ideas rehearsed in these sessions. A sincere, flowing, and persuasive argument can be presented when the advocate is comfortable with the material and the delivery.

3.20 Critique Your Summation

After constructing the closing argument, the advocate can review the following factors to determine if the argument is effective:

> Does the closing argument explain why to find for the party?
>
> Does the closing argument make the decision maker want to find for the party?
>
> Does the closing argument describe how to find for the party?
>
> Does the closing argument cover all factors that should be considered?

Advocates have difficulty constructing a closing argument that covers everything that needs to be said. Several barriers must be overcome to construct a comprehensive closing. First, the advocate who knows the case very well will have some difficulty in deciding what needs to be told. Secondly, every case has some gaps, caused by missing evidence or natural omissions, which need to be covered during closing. If not, the fact finders will create their own conclusions and inferences, which may not support the verdict or judgment requested. Thirdly, the natural curiosity of the fact finder needs to be satisfied. Information that is not legally relevant to the case may need to be discussed to make a more complete story and to satisfy the fact finder's curiosity.

In jury trials, conversations with jurors after a verdict (when permitted in a jurisdiction) sometimes reveal the jurors deliberated over matters the attorney did not consider important or were not covered in detail during the trial. Opinions written by arbitrators or administrative law judges and conversations with them after the case is over will often indicate what is important to them and what has been missed or overlooked. These situations provide an opportunity to learn from hindsight what should have been presented during the trial. The attorney should consider in advance what the fact finders may want to know, fill in these gaps, and answer potential questions during the closing argument.

One way of determining this information is to rehearse before colleagues or friends and ask them what is missing, what gaps exist, what prompts their curiosity, and what questions they have. The attorney can then present an argument that not only contains legally relevant evidence but provides the fact finders with information that is admissible and that satisfies their curiosity. For example, the evidence in a theft case may include testimony by a victim that the defendant stole her purse as she walked home after work and that she called the police immediately after the theft when she arrived at her apartment. In order to add substance to an identification, the prosecutor should permit the witness to describe what she was thinking as she was walking before her purse was taken. The experienced prosecutor would also have the victim describe how she got in her apartment if her purse, which contained her keys, was stolen. This information prevents the jurors from incorrectly filling in gaps and speculating about information that is legally irrelevant to the case.

D. HOW TO ORGANIZE

3.21 Use a Structure

Closing arguments, like all other parts of the case, must be presented in a structured manner that most effectively achieves the purposes of the closing argument. The selection of a structure depends upon the theories, facts, law, circumstances, and strategies of the case. The following are some examples of different structures:

3.21.1 Time

The closing argument can follow the chronology of the story presented during the case.

3.21.2 Flashback

The closing argument can begin with the conclusion of the story and flashback to earlier events which explain and describe what happened.

3.21.3 Undisputed and Disputed Facts

The evidence can be explained first by describing the undisputed facts and then highlighting the disputed facts, with an explanation that the facts supporting the case are what actually happened.

3.21.4 Order of Key Witnesses

If key witnesses testified in a logical or reasonable order, summation can be structured based on their testimony.

3.21.5 Issues, Positions, Topics

Summation can be structured based on the order the issues, positions, or topics were presented in a case.

3.21.6 Claims or Defenses

The structure of a closing can be based on the claims the plaintiff asserts or on the defenses the defendant asserts. A plaintiff's advocate can structure the closing to reflect the parts of claims. For example, the plaintiff in a breach of contract case can present an argument based on the factors that prove the existence of a breach of warranty. The defense may organize a final argument based on the number of defenses supported by the evidence. For example, a criminal defense attorney can present a closing argument based on a number of reasonable doubts.

3.21.7 Liability and Damages

In civil cases, the closing argument could begin with an explanation of the liability issues followed by the damage issues, or vice versa.

3.21.8 Jury Instructions, Verdict Form

In a jury trial, summation can be based on the order of the jury instructions and the verdict form. The attorney can follow the sequence of the elements of the law the judge will explain to the jury. For example, in a criminal case, the prosecutor can structure a final argument by following the elements to be proved in a burglary case. In a civil case, a verdict form that contains special interrogatories provides an organized way of reviewing the evidence. The jurors will sequentially answer these questions as they appear in the form, and counsel can use the same format during closing argument.

E.　INTRODUCING THE CLOSING

There are a number of topics that should be considered for every summation. The topics to be covered during the summation need to be structured in an orderly, persuasive manner. An example of such a structure is:

The introductory statement.

Explanation of pivotal issues in the case.

Summary of important facts, opinions, and inferences.

Description of who, what, when, where, how, and why.

Application of facts to support legal elements.

Summary of strengths of the case.

Explanation of weaknesses of opponent's case.

Reference to burden of proof.

Explanation of the law, or key jury instructions or verdict form.

Explanation of reasons why the fact finder should return favorable verdict.

Description of result sought.

Conclusion.

3.22　Introduction

The introduction sets the tone for the final argument and should be designed to have a persuasive impact. The proper tone of a case depends upon the facts and circumstances and the primary goal of the introductory statements. A common way to begin is a low-key approach, with any appeals to emotion reserved until later stages of the closing. Another approach is to establish an appropriate, emotional tone at the beginning and periodically return to this emotional theme during the closing.

The following examples demonstrate alternative introductory statements.

3.23 Case Theory Introduction

An effective way to begin the closing argument is to summarize in a few sentences the factual summaries and legal theories of the case.

Example

This case is about a job that was arbitrarily taken from a hardworking woman. This case is about Maria Elvirez and her right to be treated fairly and decently. This case is not about some abstract facts. What you heard from this witness stand and what you read from these documents really happened. It happened to this woman. It happened because of the poor judgment and mismanagement by this defendant.

Example

This lawsuit is about safety. William Blackduck had a right to the safe functioning of the products he bought from the defendant. He had a right to expect he would not be electrocuted by a defectively designed product—a tragedy that could have been prevented by inexpensive insulation. Insulation protects people against shock and could have—would have—prevented the unnecessary death of William Blackduck. A small expense—$5.00 for a ceramic insulator on the chain of this window washer's harness—would have prevented the electrocution of William Blackduck.

3.24 Dramatic Introduction

A dramatic introductory statement attempts to establish an atmosphere, set a tone, and grab attention. A dramatic statement that is appropriate to the case and presented in a sincere and natural manner can be effective.

Example (Civil Case)

What is more precious than the birth of a child? A child who is healthy and who has a full life to live. To love, to cry, to laugh, to fail, to succeed. What is more tragic than the birth of a child who is born without the ability to take care of herself, to ever tell her parents how much she loves them, to ever cry, to ever laugh, to ever fail or succeed at school or work?

Example (Criminal Case)

That man (pointing to the defendant) on the morning of August 15 walked into his garage, opened up his toolbox, and pulled out a claw hammer. That man (looking at the defendant), grasping the claw hammer in his right hand, walked from his garage, through his kitchen, up the stairway, into the bedroom of his home, and deliberately stood over his wife, who was peacefully asleep. That man, the defendant Mark LaFoe, intentionally raised that claw hammer in the air and with all his might smashed that claw hammer into the face of the woman who married him and lived with him until he ruthlessly killed her.

3.25 Outline Introduction

Summation may begin with an explanation of the outline of the presentation.

Example (Civil Case)

My presentation consists of three parts—the same three parts I discussed during opening statement. First, I will review the contract with you and show how the evidence establishes the existence of a valid and enforceable contract. Second, I will explain how the evidence clearly establishes how and why the respondent breached its contract with the claimant. Third, I will review with you all the damages my client has suffered which the respondent is obligated to pay.

3.26 Explanation of Summation for Jurors

Final argument can begin with an explanation of the purpose of summation. The advantage of these preliminary remarks is that jurors may better understand the reasons for

---

closing argument. The disadvantage of these remarks is they may not be the most effective and persuasive way to begin summation.

These introductory remarks are sometimes used because attorneys need something easy to say to reduce their nervousness, or because they have heard another attorney make similar statements, or because they have not considered alternative introductory remarks. Many attorneys prefer not to begin summation with these explanatory remarks but if they make them at all may delay making them until after they explain their case theory or use an alternative attention-grabbing statement.

Example

We are now about to come to the end of this trial. Soon you will deliberate together and reach a verdict. This part of the trial—summation—provides me with an opportunity to speak to you for the last time. What I will say to you will be consistent with what I have said to you before and with what you have heard and seen during this trial.

Example

Five days ago you knew nothing about this case. This week you have heard the testimony of several witnesses and have seen several documents. Five days ago I presented to you an opening statement—a story of what you would hear and see. Today I will summarize that evidence and explain to you how the facts and the law lead to the conclusion that my client is entitled to a verdict in this case.

3.27 Expressing Gratitude

It is customary, though often not effectively done, to thank the decision makers for their attention and time. A statement of appreciation should be sincere, brief and not patronizing. These remarks may be made at any time in the summation and should be made at a time that will increase the effectiveness of the presentation.

Example

We have now come to the stage of the trial called closing argument. The witnesses have all testified. The documents have all been introduced. We, the attorneys, are almost done. You will shortly begin your deliberations to reach a just and fair verdict in this case. My client and I, and all of us involved in this trial, thank you for the time and attention you have devoted to this case.

3.28 Defense Introductions

The defense can begin summation with any one of these suggested openings in jurisdictions where there is no rebuttal. In jurisdictions where there is rebuttal, defense follows the plaintiff/prosecutor. An alternative introductory statement may include an indirect or direct reference to a statement made by the opposition during the initial closing by the plaintiff/prosecutor.

Example (Civil Case)

You have just heard part of the story of what happened on August 1. You did not hear an explanation of the entire story. You will now, and when you do you will understand how the evidence supports the whole story told by the respondent and does not support the partial story told by the claimant.

Example (A Multiparty Case)

In some cases there are two sides to a story. In this case, there are three sides to the story. During the trial you heard and saw evidence introduced in bits and pieces supporting different versions of what happened three years ago during September. I will help you piece together the third story and show you how the bits of evidence lead you to the conclusion that it is the only accurate and reliable story of what happened.

Example (Criminal Case)

The prosecutor used this chart to explain to you the legal elements of the crime the government had to prove beyond a reasonable doubt for you to conclude that my client is guilty of burglary. I will explain to you how the prosecutor failed to prove these elements, and then I will present to you six additional reasonable doubts why John Sapphire did not commit the crime that happened on June 15.

3.29 Rebuttal Introductions

The advocate who has a rebuttal argument can begin with a prepared introductory statement or can begin with remarks that contradict defendant's argument.

Example (Criminal Case)

Defense counsel wants you to think there are six reasons which show there is reasonable doubt in this case that her client did not steal over $50,000 worth of jewelry. There are no such six reasons. The evidence clearly establishes the guilt of John Sapphire. I told you during opening statement I would present evidence to you of the guilt of John Sapphire. I presented that evidence to you. I now want to clarify a few remarks counsel made during her closing argument and answer a few questions you may have in your mind about how John Sapphire committed the crime of burglary.

3.30 Alternative Introductions

The advocate should prepare introductory remarks that most effectively meet the primary goal the advocate wants to achieve during the beginning of the closing argument. The previous examples illustrate some possibilities. Other approaches should be considered. Ideas about other introductory statements may be obtained from the world of art and literature, including plays, movies, books, or from arguments given by other advocates.

A number of alternative introductory statements may be prepared and, after selecting the most effective statement, the other introductory statements may be modified and used during some other stage of the closing argument. For example, an advocate may prefer to begin with an explanation of the case theory followed by an explanation of the purpose of closing argument. Or an advocate may prefer to begin with a dramatic statement followed by an explanation of the outline of the closing argument.

3.31 Conclusion

Summation should conclude with a strong ending. The conclusion of the argument should be well thought out and should be designed to tie the argument together and be a clear and obvious ending. The conclusion also provides one opportunity to politely and sincerely thank the decision makers for their time and attention, if not done previously. Even if there have been some problems in the argument and the advocate gets flustered or lost, a strong conclusion may help offset these problems.

Example (Criminal Case)

Roland's liberty and future are in your hands. We thank you for your time and the attention you have devoted to this case. Years from now when you look back at this trial, you must be able to conclude that your verdict was the right one, that it was fair and just. Years from now, the prosecutor may not remember this case, nor may the public. But the defendant cannot forget. Roland Sarjinna must live all his life with your decision, which can only be not guilty.

Soon you will go and deliberate. Let me tell you a story to help direct you. There was an old man and a young boy. The old man was known to be very wise. The young boy was scheming of a way to prove that the old man was not wise about everything. And so the young boy trapped a little bird, and he took it in his hands and went up to the old man. He said, "Old man, old man, what do I have in my hands?" And the old man, being wise, said, "You have a little bird." And the clever little boy said, "Tell me, old man, is the bird alive or dead?" And the young boy gleefully thought, "Now I have him. For you see, if the old man says it is alive, I will crush it and kill it and show him that it was dead. And if the old man says it is dead, I will open my hands and turn the little bird free, proving the old man is wrong." And the old man, being very wise, looked at the clever little boy straight in the eyes and said, "The answer is in your hands." And the liberty and future of Roland Sarjinna is now in your hands.

Example (Rebuttal)

The defense has asked you to find his client not guilty and send him home to live his life. The defense spoke on behalf of his client who sits here in the courtroom. But there is another person who is not here. Her life came to a brutal end by the hands of the man who now asks you for mercy, who now asks to go home. Where is the mercy he showed for Priscilla Hoskins? She will never go home. She will never see her six-year-old child. Who will speak for her? Members of the Jury, you will speak for her when you return the only verdict supported by the facts and law in the case: a verdict of guilty of murder in the first degree.

Example (Civil Case)

I'm going to close now. Defense counsel for Axon Corporation told you a number of times that you were not to decide this case based on sympathy you might have in this case for Tracy Valhalla. It would be natural for you to have sympathetic feelings for Ms. Valhalla, who told you in this hearing how she is struggling to maintain the operation of her neighborhood service station that she has worked hard to maintain for 10 years. Your Honor, Tracy Valhalla does not want your sympathy. Her family and friends can sympathize with her. You should not and need not decide this case based upon sympathy. Ms. Valhalla wants only what she is legally entitled to under the facts of this case. She has a right to the defendant's money, the money that they owe her under the franchise agreement. Tracy Valhalla deserves an award in the amount of $875,000, an amount supported not by sympathy, but by the facts and the law.

F. TELL A STORY

One of the primary goals of closing argument is for the advocate to provide reasons that support a favorable result. The advocate has broad latitude in explaining these reasons which are based on the theories of the case, facts and opinions, inferences and conclusions, and the law applicable to the case.

This section lists many factors to consider when developing the final argument. The factors have been organized into seven categories for ease of analysis and application. These categories are:

Argument.

Evidence.

Law.

Techniques.

Tactical considerations.

Criminal cases.

Civil cases.

The advocate must consider which of these factors should be included and how they should be organized and presented in summation. Some factors may be inappropriate in arguments before judges and arbitrators. Some factors—such as explaining the evidence and the law—will be included in all closings, while the inclusion of others will be discretionary.

3.32 Examples of Arguments

The closing argument allows an advocate to say most any reasonable thing that falls within the broad definition of argument. An advocate may:

(A) Draw Reasonable Inferences From Direct or Circumstantial Evidence

Example

My client, Henry Balzar, received a hand-delivered letter at his home from the plaintiff at about 6 p.m. on February 20. The plaintiff claims Henry threatened his life on that very day. I'm sure you will agree that someone supposedly in fear for his life is not going to hand-deliver a letter to his enemy's home after a supposed threat was made. What can we infer from these circumstances? The plaintiff's charge of assault is not supported by the facts.

(B) Suggest That Certain Evidence Implies a Reasonable Conclusion

Example

The facts that Summit State Bank hired five part-time file clerks, that the manager took Marnie Alexander off her regular duties once the high school students were trained and put Marnie to work cleaning the office—a task degrading and not related to Marnie's job—and that Marnie was laid off during the same week two additional part-timers were hired all suggest one conclusion: Summit State Bank wanted to get rid of Marnie Alexander.

(C) Present Conclusions Based Upon the Circumstances of the Case

Example

Arthur Bach had drunk nearly a fifth of bourbon during the snowstorm. He had a cigarette in his mouth when he poured gasoline from a five gallon canister into the fuel tank of the Blizzard Snowblower. Arthur Bach failed to take adequate or reasonable steps for his own safety when he tragically and accidently killed himself.

(D) Suggest That the Decision Makers Apply Common Sense in Deciding a Case

Example

You are to use your common sense when deciding this case. You are to rely upon your common sense in deciding how probable and how likely is the plaintiff's story. You are to use your common sense in concluding how unlikely and untrue the defense story is in this case. And when you do, you will reject the coincidences the defendant wants you to believe.

(E) Suggest That the Decision Makers Apply Their Common Sense and Life Experiences in Determining a Fact

Example

You know what it means in this society to be attractive. You know you cannot tell Rita Riley that her scars don't matter. Everything Rita confronts in life will remind her she is scarred—that she is not attractive. You know what value our society places on physical beauty. Rita will never meet another human being face-to-face without that other person's face reflecting the horror of her disfigurement.

(F) Unabashedly Pleading for Mercy

Example

This is my first and may be my last case, and I'd like to go out a winner.

3.33 Summarize The Story

The explanation of the facts may be told in a story form which includes descriptions of the scene, the characters, and the event. The goal should be to summarize facts in a way that is reasonable and consistent with the recollection of the fact finder. The advocate should keep in mind that the fact finder has heard the evidence and need to be accurately reminded of the facts, not misled by inaccurate argument.

Example (Civil Case)

Marnie Alexander began working part-time for Massasoit Bank when she was 55 years old in order to supplement her husband's income. Walter Alexander's income was severely cut back because of his retirement due to a partial knee replacement. Marnie's work was praised; she received substantial raises each review period. But then Massasoit Bank was taken over by Summit State Bank. Suddenly Marnie was pressured into working nearly eight hours a day. Next Marnie was given degrading tasks to do, such as cleaning the office—tasks having nothing to do with her skills as a filing clerk. Finally, Marnie was ordered to train in three young students, two of whom were still in high school. After these girls were trained, Marnie was laid off. Why? Because Marnie is 63 years old. Summit State Bank has never recalled Marnie to work. Instead Summit State Bank has hired two more part-time high school students.

3.34 Explain Why Something Happened

The evidence presented may tell what happened and how something happened. The advocate may need to explain why something happened.

Example (Civil Case)

You have heard the evidence in this case and you know what happened during the surgery and how Dr. Kildare conducted that surgery. You must decide why Dr. Kildare performed the surgery the way he did. The evidence leads you to only one conclusion: Dr. Kildare was negligent. He made a mistake. Even though he is a doctor, he is still a human, and he made a serious mistake. He did not intend to hurt my client. He did not plan to make a mistake, but he did.

3.35 Describe the Evidence

A substantial part of a closing argument consists of the advocate summarizing and explaining the evidence. This description should be consistent both with the facts described in the opening statement and with the evidence produced during the case.

Example

I do not intend to argue but rather explain the evidence to you. Time does not allow me to cover every bit of testimony, every piece of evidence, or every exhibit. I may not mention some things that you recall, but I am sure you will remember those matters. Now I would like to summarize the evidence you have heard and seen.

3.36 Present the Witnesses

The advocate may summarize the evidence by identifying the witnesses who testified to certain facts and opinions. Witnesses who were especially effective, persuasive, or credible should be referred to by name. If a case involves a large number of witnesses who testify over a lengthy period of time, the advocate needs to not only identify the witness by name but also establish when they testified and the topics of their testimony.

Example (Civil Case)

We brought before you the testimony of the two people who talked to each other in the phone conversation on October 15. First, there was Louis Armstrong. Mr. Armstrong was the manager of the Cosmos Band. He took the stand and told you he had been managing the band for two years and during that October 15 telephone conversation he told Frank Hester the band was available to play on New Year's Eve. After he testified, Frank Hester testified. Mr. Hester was the manager of the Sylvan Lounge. Mr. Hester told you it was his job to contract with bands to play at the lounge. He also told you Louis Armstrong told him in that same telephone conversation on October 15 that the Cosmos Band was available to play on New Year's Eve.

3.37 Explain the Credibility of Witnesses

An advocate may comment on the credibility of a witness, may demonstrate how an observation or statement is inaccurate, may attempt to show a witness is biased or prejudiced, or may comment on the witness' demeanor. Impeachment techniques may be used during the case to establish facts to reduce that witness' credibility. The advocate can restate the facts developed on cross-examination, which establishes why a witness should not be believed, or that a witness' perceptions are improbable or implausible.

Example (Lie)

You heard the plaintiff's boss, Maxwell Higgins, testify that he fired the plaintiff because the plaintiff lied on his employment application. The plaintiff had lied on that application not once but on every page. Page one, the plaintiff was not honorably discharged from the Marines, he was never a Marine. Page two, the plaintiff was not laid off from the Forest Community College, he was fired for sexually harassing students. Page three, the plaintiff did not receive a Ph.D in linguistics from LaSalle University, the plaintiff's last degree was a B.A. in speech and communication from Hampton College. Plaintiff is not an honest or honorable person in his professional or personal life.

Example (Mistake)

There are two key witnesses who testified for the plaintiff. Rosencrantz and Guildenstern both testified that they saw an accident. You have to determine whether they saw what they say they saw. There are several factors which influence the ability of an eye-witness to see what actually happened. One factor is how close they were to the scene of the accident. Another factor is how clear a line of vision they had of the accident. Another is what they were doing immediately before the accident. Let's apply those three factors to the testimony of Rosencrantz and Guildenstern.

Example (Demeanor)

One of the factors you can consider in determining the credibility of Ms. loto is her demeanor during direct and cross-examination. Did she appear to be telling the truth? Did she seem uncertain? Was she evasive? During her direct examination, she appeared to be uncertain about the time of the day she met with the defendant in her office. Counsel for defendant had to suggest the answer to her. If she was uncertain about that key piece of evidence, perhaps she was uncertain about other matters.

During her cross-examination, when I asked her questions, her attitude changed, and her memory became worse. She was not as cooperative in answering my questions and giving you information the way she was when she answered questions asked by opposing counsel. She remembered fewer details about conversations she had with her supervisor, the person for whom she is still working.

Example (Relationship)

We all heard the testimony of the defendant's wife. We all heard her testify in direct examination that her husband was with her the entire evening when the crime was committed. We all heard her testify in cross-examination that she loved her husband very much and continues to love him very much.

There is nothing more beautiful than the bond that exists between a loving wife and husband. There is no doubt that Mrs. James loved her husband before the murder, and that she loves him after the murder. She loves him because he is her husband. She loves him even though he is a murderer. And she naturally wants to give him an alibi and tell you he was with her when he committed the murder. She would rather violate her oath to tell the truth than have you find him guilty.

3.38 Describe Circumstantial Evidence

Evidence presented in the case consists of direct and circumstantial evidence. The concept of circumstantial evidence is difficult to understand. Jurors and the judge or arbitrator need to be told how important and valuable or how weak this evidence is.

Example

Circumstantial evidence has the same value as direct evidence. An example of circumstantial evidence that demonstrates how accurate and compelling it is, is the story of Robinson Crusoe. You recall that Crusoe was on an island and he thought he was all alone. One morning he went down to the beach and he saw a footprint on the sand. Knowing that someone else was on the island, he became so overcome with emotion that he fainted. He didn't see anyone, but he knew because of the footprint there was someone else on the island. He woke to find Friday, the person who made the footprint, standing beside him, who was to be his friend on the island. The footprint—the marks on the sand made by a human foot—was circumstantial evidence. His seeing Friday was direct evidence. Both were true and compelling. Let's look at the facts of this case—the footprints that tell us what happened.

Example (Criminal Case)

There is no direct evidence in this case which links my client to the crime. The prosecution has used circumstantial evidence in an effort to prove to you the guilt of my client, but that evidence proves nothing. You know how weak, inaccurate, and misleading this type of evidence is. Some of you may recall the story from the Bible regarding Joseph and his brothers. Joseph was the favorite son of his father, Jacob. His brothers were very envious of him and they beat him and sold him into slavery. They wanted their father to believe that Joseph was dead, and so they took Joseph's coat and some goat's blood, and they smeared the goat's blood on the coat, and showed the coat to their father who concluded that Joseph had been killed by some evil beast. Of course, the truth was that Joseph was alive, but his father believed him to be dead. And so it is in this case. The truth is my client is innocent, but the prosecution attempts to convince you that he is guilty. You cannot rely on the weak circumstantial evidence in this case to find my client guilty. If you did, you would be making the same tragic mistake that Joseph's father did.

3.39 Present Detail and Corroboration

A detailed factual explanation has the advantage of explaining the relationship between various types of evidence that may not have been obvious or made clear during the case. Summation provides an opportunity for the advocate to explain the primary source of the facts and to describe sources of circumstantial evidence and corroborating facts. This explanation will increase the persuasiveness of the evidence by explaining the connection between facts which the fact finder may have missed.

Example

My client is not liable for the tragic death of Hank Tudor because the facts show Mr. Tudor was not using reasonable care for his own safety. You heard testimony from Mr. Wolsey, a friend of Mr. Tudor, that Mr. Tudor didn't know how to use the all-terrain vehicle, and that Mr. Tudor put the owner's manual—still in its unbroken plastic seal—on the shelf of the garage. Mr. Tudor's wife, Catherine, testified that Defense

Exhibit No. 6, the owner's manual, taken from the Tudor's garage, remains unopened, just as Mr. Tudor had left it. You also heard Tom Cromwell, Mr. Tudor's neighbor, testify that after Mr. Tudor started the ATV, he said to Mr. Cromwell, "Well, here goes. I want to see how fast this thing can go."

3.40 Refer to Actual Evidence

The factual explanation may employ words used by the witnesses or words that appear in documents. The advocate should neither overstate nor understate the facts. Quoting the testimony of a witness and mixing that quote with a factual summary is often an effective approach. Reading testimony from a transcript of the case can also be very persuasive. Reading from an exhibit or showing highlighted portions of the exhibit can be equally effective.

Example (Criminal Case)

Yesterday you heard Pam Falzone testify about meeting Joe Wiley after the Alinisi poetry reading. She testified that Joe admitted his part in the crime. This transcript—which you heard yesterday—of what Joe said proves what he did:

Q: When did you next see Joe?

A: He picked me up right after my economics class, about 3:30.

Q: What did you do when you were driving?

A: I talked about my day. I mentioned that I was in Jordan Auditorium waiting for Alinisi to arrive for a poetry reading, when all of a sudden three police officers came in and told us to go down to the lobby.

Q: After you told him what happened, what was his reaction?

A: He laughed so hard he had to pull over to the side of the road. He said at 12:45, just before the 1:00 reading was scheduled, he called Carol, the secretary and threatened that a bomb would go off in Jordan Auditorium if Alinisi went ahead with the reading.

No reasonable person makes an admission like that unless he did what he admitted he did. Joe wanted to impress Pam. He wanted her to share in his secret.

G. SUMMATION TO A JURY

3.41 Explain the Law in Jury Trials

The judge will explain the law during final jury instructions. An attorney must summarize and explain pivotal instructions, and must accurately state the content of the instructions. The attorney can read from or quote the exact jury instructions. Many instructions will not adequately or clearly explain the law because the instructions contain abstract legal concepts. In these situations, the attorney may comment on the instructions and provide an expanded (and correct) description of the instruction and of its meaning in simple, easy-to-understand language.

An accurate explanation of jury instructions can be very persuasive. The final instructions come from the judge, whom the jurors usually respect and understand to be impartial and the source of the law. Jurors are likely to be persuaded by an explanation by a trial attorney that is supported by the instructions. A copy of the jury instructions is often given to the jurors for use during deliberations, and an argument based upon these instructions will more likely be remembered and discussed by the jurors.

Example (Civil Trial)

The law provides you with legal guidelines and explanations to guide you and assist you in reaching a verdict. These explanations are called instructions on the law. The judge has explained some of them to you already. The judge will explain more of them to you after we have completed our summation.

Now I would like to discuss with you how those instructions apply to this case.

This is a negligence case. The judge will tell you what negligence is and the judge will also tell you what it is not. The court will tell you, and I am quoting what the court will tell you:

Negligence is lack of ordinary care. It is the failure to exercise that degree of care which a reasonably prudent or careful person would have exercised under the same circumstance.

That is the standard. That is the law: A person must do what a reasonable person would do under the circumstances of the case. Otherwise that person is negligent. And that person in this case is the defendant.

3.42　Describe Special Interrogatories

A case may involve special interrogatories which require the jury to make specific findings of fact during deliberations. These interrogatories may accompany a general or special verdict. The attorney may read special interrogatories to the jury and urge the jurors to answer in a specific way. The applicable law will determine whether an attorney can inform the jury that the answers to any one of the interrogatories may determine the outcome of the case. In most cases, the attorney can comment upon the effect of special interrogatories.

Example (Civil Trial)

There are several things the plaintiff has to prove to you before you can hold my client responsible for what happened in this case. To help you decide who is responsible for what happened, you will be given a list of questions you must answer in the jury room. The judge will give you those questions on a sheet of paper. I've had the piece of paper enlarged so that we can go through these questions together to discuss how these questions should be answered. Let me place this on the easel.

The first question is: "Did the plaintiff and the defendant enter into a contract on May 1? ___ Yes, ___ No." The judge will explain the elements that make up a contract. I've also had that explanation enlarged on this board. Let's apply the facts that all of us heard in this case to these elements to determine if a contract was entered into.

3.43 Explain the Jury System

In jury trials, it is common for one or both attorneys to explain the purpose the jury serves in our system of justice and the importance of the jury's decision. These appeals, if done sincerely, can be effective.

Example (Power of the Jury)

As jurors you are part of a tradition that is hundreds of years old. You are members of the community who come together and decide significant cases like this. Individually you are each a citizen. Collectively sitting here as jurors you are part of our system of justice. You hold in your hands the power to judge the difference between right and wrong. Today you will exercise that power to set right what has been done wrong.

Example (Conscience of the Community)

Jurors, you are the conscience of the community. When you speak, the community speaks. You represent this community and its conscience and its attitudes. You shape and form the conscience of our community through your decision.

3.44 Request a Verdict

A closing argument must include an explanation of the specific verdict the attorney wants for the client. This explanation should be clear so the jurors understand what conclusion they must reach to find for a party. In most cases, the request will be a specific request for a verdict of guilty or not guilty or for a verdict for the plaintiff or defendant.

Example

When you reach your verdict you must think it through and understand what it means. Verdict is a latin word meaning to speak the truth, so by your verdict you are going to speak the truth here today. Once you write down your verdict, no one can change it. You can't be called back and told, "That's not right. You didn't do it right. Do it again." What you do here today is done forever.

It is also important that you reach your verdict for the right reason. Not only should the result be right—it is just as important that the reasons for it are right.

You may find for the defendant in this case, and your verdict might be correct. But if your reason for finding in her favor is because you are concerned about her reputation or about her future, then your reason would have been wrong. You may only find in her favor if she did not breach this contract. If you found she breached the contract, then any other reason that you might think of as to why you ought to find in her favor would be a wrong reason—would constitute an injustice.

You may find for the plaintiff. And we believe you will. And your verdict will be correct because the defendant breached this contract.

H. USE PERSUASIVE TECHNIQUES

3.45 Use Analogies, Metaphors, Anecdotes

The advocate may wish to refer to analogous situations, or use metaphors or tell an anecdotal story to make a point during summation. The images described through an analogy, a metaphor, or anecdote may assist the fact finder in understanding the point of law or application of fact to law. While a carefully drawn, common sense metaphor or analogy may assist in understanding a concept, careful consideration should be given before one is used. If the analogy or metaphor is too simple or does not make sense, the point will not be made with persuasive impact. If there is an opportunity for the opponent to argue following the presentation of an analogy or metaphor, the opponent could make the use of these techniques appear simplistic or foolish.

Example

They left a time bomb ticking at Palmetto Estates. It was just a matter of time before Jenkins would use his master key to get into Kathy Fermon's apartment. It was just a matter of time before Jenkins would renew his acts of terror. That time struck on May 15 when Jenkins, hiding in Kathy's kitchen, surprised her, held a knife to her throat and brutally assaulted her. The people of Palmetto Estates lit that fuse and started that time bomb ticking when they negligently hired Jenkins on the basis of his letter with no references and no prior dates or places of employment. Even when the secretary of the Palmetto Board of Directors found Jenkins in a drunken and disorderly state and reported this to the Board, the Board did nothing. The Board could have defused the situation and spared Kathy Fermon, but the Board did not make the one phone call to the police that would have stopped the disaster. One phone call would have informed Palmetto Estates that Jenkins was on parole for another assault. But the Board did not take the time to investigate and fire Jenkins, and that was all the time Jenkins needed. They are responsible for Jenkins exploding.

Example (Plaintiff's Attorney)

The agreement between Jo Jacobs and Health Center, Incorporated was like a web. Doctor Jacobs, just finished with a residency, wanted to begin her pediatric practice. Health Center required her to sign an employment contract according to its terms: if she ever wanted to leave Health Center, she could not practice in a 100 mile radius of Clarendon for five years. She knew she wanted to begin a practice in Clarendon. What she didn't know was that Health Center, Incorporated was not the kind of practice she wanted.

After three months, Jo Jacobs resigned. She was caught in a web and she couldn't pull away. The more she struggled and tried to reason with Health Center's administration, the more menacingly loomed the spider.

When Jo Jacobs ventured from Health Center, she started her own office in Clarendon. The spider let her build up a practice and then flung out the web again. An injunction closed her office and stopped her from earning a livelihood to support herself and her six-year-old son in their modest home. She is unable to practice; her medical school loans are in default; her mortgage payments are overdue. Health Center, like a spider that stores up victims for later consumption, wrapped Jo Jacobs in its web as an example for the rest of its employees.

Example (Defendant's Lawyer)

Members of the Jury, counsel has spent a lot of time talking about voracious spiders and sinister webs. Let's consider the reality. Doctor Joanne Jacobs is a competent, well-educated adult. She knew what she was doing when she signed her employment contract. Society, and you, must hold her responsible for her obligations. There is nothing menacing about Health Center. The center provides a vital service to the Clarendon community.

3.46　Be Creative

One of the primary tasks of the advocate in closing argument is to be creative and innovative and explain the significance of inferences. While the direct and circumstantial evidence may lead to clear and obvious conclusions, the advocate's task is to explain the less obvious conclusions. The advocate needs to highlight the subtle nuances of the facts presented.

Example

(*Assume that the defendant is accused of assaulting the victim in an alley one block away from a bar where the defendant and victim had a fight.*)

My client, Fred Allen, has been accused of hiding in an alley, waiting for the victim to pass so that he could jump out and attack the victim because of something that happened in the bar. My client did not hide in that alley, did not jump out, did not attack the victim. It was somebody else. We don't know who or why, but it was somebody else.

You recall that the victim, Jack Benny, said that he had never met my client before that night, did not know where my client lived, and did not tell my client where he lived. And you recall that Mr. Benny said he and my client never talked before or after their argument in the bar, except to call each other names and yell at each other.

You also recall during my cross-examination of Mr. Benny, he told us that when he left the bar he could have left through the rear door on Mason Street, or he could have gone out through the front door and turned left and walked west toward Dixie Street, or could have gone through the front door and crossed the street toward Main Street. Instead, he testified that he went out through the front door and turned right toward Richmond Avenue.

You may have wondered why I asked those questions. His answers tell us that my client is innocent and did not assault him. My client, Mr. Allen, did not know where Mr. Benny lived. My client did not know which way Mr. Benny would leave when he left the bar that night. My client would not know to hide in a dark alley one block east on Richmond Avenue. There was no way my client would have known whether the victim would have left the bar through the front or the rear doors or which way the victim would have walked home—because my client did not know where the victim lived. Some stranger was waiting in that alley, ready to attack anyone who passed by. Mr. Benny was that unfortunate person who happened to pass by. Mr. Benny was tragically attacked by that stranger while my client was on his way home in a bus.

3.47 Use Exhibits

The design, placement, and use in the argument are as important as the actual visual aid or exhibit itself. The importance of the exhibit in the case, the impact words and colors on the visual aids, the location in the room for clear viewing and easy access, the placement in the structure of the presentation, and the style of the advocate in the use of and reference to the exhibit are important considerations in determining whether the exhibit will aid or interfere with the final argument presentation.

Example (Exhibit)

The most critical piece of evidence in this case did not come from that witness stand, and did not come from the testimony of witnesses. The most critical piece of evidence is contained in Plaintiff's Exhibit No. 1, this letter written by the defendant to plaintiff's employer. This letter was read to you during the trial, and each of you individually had an opportunity to read it yourself. We had this letter enlarged so that we can go over what the defendant wrote in that letter, and focus on the meaning of the words the defendant used.

Example (Visual Aid)

Over the past two weeks of trial, you have heard from many witnesses and reviewed many documents. The judge will tell you that you must find my client not guilty if, based on all that evidence, you have a reasonable doubt that he committed a crime. The evidence in this case reveals there are at least ten reasonable doubts. We have prepared a chart which lists those ten reasonable doubts and the supporting evidence.

3.48 Personalize Experiences

It can be helpful during summation to mention situations the fact finder might have experienced that resemble what happened in the case. For example, if the issue in a case is the eyewitness identification of the defendant, and the theory is that the witness misidentified the defendant, the advocate for the defendant can suggest this happens in other situations in life.

Example

Have you ever been at a party and saw someone across the room and recognized them as a friend, only to approach that person and find out that it was not your friend, even though it looked like your friend from a distance? Have you ever been at a restaurant and called for your waiter only to be embarrassed because the person you called was not your waiter, even though you had seen him and talked with him several times? The witness here similarly picked out the wrong person. And that is perfectly understandable. The witness here was scared and frightened and did not expect to confront a stranger. At a party or at a restaurant that fear is not there. Reasonable people make many mistakes in identifying friends or people they meet. And the witness made the same mistake in this case.

3.49 Appeal to Reason and Emotion

Summation may include appeals both to reason and to emotion. An explanation of the facts and law can support a logical reason why a party is entitled to a favorable result. An appeal to emotion may create a motivating force to support a decision based on reason and logic. An approach that blends these two factors increases the chances of a successful result.

The extent to which an advocate relies upon both emotion and logic for an argument depends upon the circumstances of a case. With some cases it will be more effective to emphasize a rational, logical explanation of the evidence and the law. In other cases, it will be more effective to rely on the emotions and feelings created by the facts. An advocate must carefully balance the use of emotion in a case.

Two common basic emotions are like and dislike. Appeals to emotions during summation can be based on these two feelings. Generating a feeling of dislike or hate toward a party sufficient to support a result against that party will be difficult, unless the facts justify such an attack. The positive emotion will be easier to establish on behalf of a client to persuade the fact finder that a party is entitled to a victory. The more effective argument is to show that a person is entitled to the benefit of a favorable result, rather than trying to show that a person ought to be punished by losing a case.

Example (Liability)

We all have feelings for what happened. Those feelings are natural and appropriate. You should use those feelings in your evaluation of the facts of this case. Only humans can understand and appreciate the facts of this case. You are to rely on your feelings of empathy just as you are to use your reasoning in deciding this case.

Example (Damages)

Counsel for defendant has told you that there are some expenses Mr. and Mrs. O'Connor will not incur as a result of Danny's death, that there is some money they will not have to spend on their dead son. That is true. There are also some things they will never have to put up with because Danny is no longer with them. They will never have to sit in the heat of the sun on a hot, July afternoon, watching Danny play Little League baseball. They will never have to wait in long lines in some crowded toy store before the hectic days of Christmas buying Danny some toy that will break the day after Christmas. They will never have to lay awake at night, worrying about where their teenage son is and why he isn't home. They will not have to live through all that.

3.50 Ask Rhetorical Questions

A rhetorical question can be an effective tool of persuasion because it directly involves the decision maker in the presentation. The essential aspect of a rhetorical question is that the answer should be obvious. Rhetorical questions cause problems when the fact finder answers them differently than the advocate. If the advocate believes the decision maker may not answer the rhetorical question the same way the advocate would, the rhetorical question should be answered immediately for the fact finder.

Example (Counsel Holding Photograph)

Mr. Montana is scarred. He is disfigured. His hands and arms will require grafting and plastic surgery. Can anyone look at this picture and fail to see years of anguish—emotional and physical—for Mr. Montana?

Example

Was Garfield House Apartments negligent in inspecting and maintaining the Ruud water heater? There is only one answer: No! Garfield House Apartments not only had a maintenance manager periodically check the system but also had a service contract to cover any repairs.

I. BE POSITIVE ABOUT NEGATIVES

3.51 Explain Contradictions

It will be obvious a dispute exists between the parties. What will not always be obvious, however, is the specific factual contradictions in the case. Some cases do not involve apparent factual differences but involve subtle contrary inferences and conclusions. The advocate may need to highlight the inconsistencies between witnesses, to point out the contradictions in testimony.

Example

The issue in this case you must decide is whether a telephone conversation took place on May 2. The plaintiffs have raised another issue—a side issue which is not relevant to the merits of this case. That side issue might misdirect you from focusing on the real issue in this case. That misdirection is a magician's tool, a magic trick. And like a magic trick, that side issue is an illusion. It is not the real issue in this case.

3.52 Comment on Case Weaknesses

Every case will have some weak points which must be addressed in closing argument. If an advocate can think of a reasonable interpretation that reduces the obvious weakness of a point, that explanation should be provided. If the advocate cannot think of any mitigating explanation, then the weakness should be conceded in a candid and forthright manner. This disclosure may enhance the credibility of the advocate and reduce the impact of the opposition's focus on such weakness.

Example (Civil Case)

It may not have been a good idea to let a six-year-old child ride a full-sized ten-speed bicycle. But, Dennis was ecstatic with his birthday present. Nothing could have kept that child from trying out that bike. His parents—preoccupied with the three-week-old baby and Dennis' birthday guests—couldn't have known Dennis was taking that bike onto the county road instead of the long farm driveway where he always rode his old bicycle.

3.53 Attack the Opposition's Positions

An effective technique may be to attack the logic and reasonableness of the opponent's contentions. An advocate may select one or more specific arguments of the opponent, demonstrate the weakness of the evidence or contentions, and explain how this information must be reconciled in favor of the advocate's client.

A significant portion of the closing argument should not be spent defensively responding to the opponent's issues, positions, and argument because the advocate may be perceived as not having any substantial positions. Arguments that attack the opponent's case must be balanced with arguments that support the case.

Example (Civil Case)

Counsel has tried to tell you how reasonable the substantial restrictions in Dr. Jacobs' contract with Health Center, Incorporated were. Let's review how unreasonable those restrictions really are. Five years of no practice within a 100 mile radius of Clarendon means that Dr. Jacobs would have to terminate her credentials with United Hospital, would have to end the more than 50 doctor/patient relationships she has developed with people in this community who looked to her for aid and comfort, would lose the goodwill from her medical practice that she has developed over the past four years, and would leave this community short of a highly capable, very experienced general practitioner. Those restrictions are not reasonable.

3.54 Mention Negative Suggestions

The opposition's case may have some weaknesses that ought not to be used as a reason why the opponent should lose. These weaknesses may not be sufficiently relevant or material to be a significant point, or it may not be tactful to rely on a weakness because the decision maker may perceive the reliance to be a "cheap shot." For example, if an opponent in a contract case is a recovering alcoholic, it would be folly to use that former lifestyle as a reason why the opponent should lose. However, there are some weaknesses that can be briefly mentioned during summation that tactfully remind the fact finder of some problems. This approach may work if the comments are presented in a way the fact finder does not view as unfair or sarcastic.

Example (Civil Case)

You do not need to rely on other problems with the testimony of the plaintiff's major witness, Finley Dunne, to disbelieve his story. You need not consider the fact that he drove away immediately after the accident to get to the baseball game on time and did not stop to leave his name as a witness. You can disregard the fact he did not call the police until one week after the accident to tell what he says he saw. And you can ignore the fact he refused to talk to our investigator when she called and asked him some questions about the accident and that he willingly talked to counsel for the plaintiff. But, you can't ignore the fact that Finley Dunne could not have seen what he said he saw.

3.55 Identify Broken Promises

During opening statement the opponent may have made some promise which has not been met. During closing argument the advocate should review statements made during the opening and inform the decision maker that the opponent failed to do what was promised.

Example (Civil Case)

During this case, counsel for Dennis Burdock promised to prove the Schwann bicycle was unreasonably dangerous. All counsel has shown you is that it was unreasonable for Dennis' parents to let a child ride a full-sized ten-speed bicycle, unsupervised on a road where vehicles travelled at 55 miles an hour—and more—in both lanes. And that is part of the tragedy.

3.56 Explain Absent Evidence/Witnesses

During closing argument an advocate may comment on facts which were described by the opponent during the opening statement, but that were not proven during the course of the case. If the opposition has failed to offer evidence or introduce exhibits, an attorney may comment on the significance of that non-evidence. If a party could have called a witness, if that witness could have been subpoenaed, and if that witness was a material witness, an attorney may comment on the failure of the party to call such a witness. The failure of a party to call a witness may create an inference that the witness would have testified adversely to that party.

Some situations may prohibit comments about the lack of certain evidence. For example, it is unconstitutional for a prosecutor to comment on the criminal defendant's failure to testify. It may also be improper for a party to comment on the lack of certain evidence if that information is protected by a privilege.

Example (Civil Case)

Counsel for plaintiff told you they would prove to you the defendant committed discriminatory acts against the plaintiff. Counsel for plaintiff told you they would prove the defendant made racist statements. How did they try to prove that to you? Did they call one single witness to come to this courtroom and say they heard the defendant make racist statements? No. Did they bring before you one written piece of evidence containing any racist statement by the defendant directed to the plaintiff? No. It is not enough in our system of justice for somebody to claim something happened. It is not enough in our system for someone to say they will prove to you that something happened. Our system requires the facts be brought before you so you can determine what happened. Those facts were not brought before you, and the only reasonable conclusion you can reach is, what the plaintiffs say happened did not happen.

3.57 Explain Lies vs. Mistake

Every case involves contradictory evidence pitting the testimony of one witness against another. Few witnesses actually deserve to be called a liar. More often, a better tactic is to describe a witness as being mistaken about a fact. It may be sufficient to point out that everyone sees an event from different perspectives and that how the witness has perceived an event may be a mistaken observation based on an incorrect perspective.

When claiming that a witness has lied or is mistaken, an advocate should provide a reason why that person is lying or is mistaken. Merely asserting that a witness has made an intentional or negligent mistake is not enough. The facts established on the cross-examination of that witness must be summarized to demonstrate that witness' lack of credibility.

Example (Civil Case)

Diane Turgenet told you under oath the salesperson said the warranty would cover all major mechanical problems with the car. You then heard from the salesperson, who denied making that statement to Ms. Turgenet. You have to decide whether that statement was made. Diane Turgenet remembers it was made because it was a very important factor in her decision to buy that car. Does the salesperson really remember what he said? You can easily conclude he is mistaken in what he remembers. He told you he has sold hundreds of cars and has talked to many hundreds of customers. He has no reason to remember what he told Ms. Turgenet when she asked him specific questions that were important to her about the warranty.

3.58 Anticipate Rebuttal Argument

In a jurisdiction where the party with the burden has an opportunity for rebuttal, the defense may need to explain that there will be no opportunity to counter what the opposing party will say during the last closing argument.

Example (Civil Case)

Because the plaintiff has the burden of proof in this case, the plaintiff has the opportunity to again present an argument after I have finished. I anticipate plaintiff will question the ability of Ahmad Maki to identify the truck involved in the accident. As you listen to plaintiff's counsel you should ask yourself whether what the plaintiff argues to you about the identification is supported by the evidence you heard in this case or whether it is clear Mr. Maki saw that truck. I will not have another opportunity to talk to you after plaintiff completes her closing argument, but I am confident you will believe Mr. Maki and not counsel's argument.

J. SUMMATION IN A CRIMINAL CASE

3.59 Describe the Criminal Burden of Proof

Both the prosecution and the defense may explain "beyond a reasonable doubt" burden of proof.

Example (Prosecution)

The term beyond a reasonable doubt does not mean proof beyond a shadow of a doubt or beyond all doubt. The prosecution need not remove all doubt in order to convict the defendant, for if that were the standard, convictions of criminals would be almost impossible.

The term "reasonable doubt" only applies to the elements of the crime that must be proved. If you have a doubt that is unreasonable, the defendant must be found guilty. If you have a doubt as to something that is not part of an element that needs to be proved, the defendant must also be found guilty. In this case, there is no reasonable doubt as to any of the elements of the crime of robbery.

Example (Defense)

The judge will tell you that a reasonable doubt is a doubt that would cause a person to pause in making an important decision or transaction in life. For example, an important decision is the purchase of a house. Imagine that the three witnesses for the prosecution are real estate agents selling a home and that the buyer of the home learns that one of the salespersons has never seen the home, another salesperson lied both to the police and under oath to a judge, and another salesperson is a convicted felon. A reasonable buyer would pause in entering into that transaction, reasonably doubt the accuracy of the statements made by those salespeople, and decide not to buy the house. Similarly, you should reasonably doubt and reject the testimony of the three witnesses for the prosecution and decide the defendant is not guilty.

3.60 Comment on Lesser Included Criminal Offenses

Lesser included offenses are difficult to explain without diminishing the strength of the argument in support of the most serious offense or of an acquittal on all charges. A prosecutor may have to decide how to deliver an argument seeking a premeditated murder conviction and, in the same argument, explain the elements of manslaughter. The defense must consider how to reduce the chances the judge or jury will find a defendant guilty of premeditated murder and at the same time not concede a conviction based on manslaughter.

Example

We have proved the defendant committed the crime of murder in the first degree. He killed his business partner with premeditation and with intent. In this case, just like many others, there are other crimes involved. They are called lesser included offenses. When we proved murder in the first degree, we also proved these additional crimes.

K. SUMMATION IN A CIVIL CASE

3.61 Describe the Civil Burden of Proof

Counsel for both plaintiff and defendant must decide whether to discuss or describe the burden of proof. In jury trials, many jurors may confuse the burden of proof in a civil case with the burden of proof in criminal cases and think that the phrase "beyond a reasonable doubt" (which they have heard countless times in movies, books, and television) should apply. The plaintiff's attorney should make certain the jury does not confuse the applicable burden of proof. In some civil cases the burden of proof is the "clear and convincing" standard.

The use of the "scales of justice" is may be effective because the description provides a visual explanation of an abstract concept and because the jurors have not previously heard this description. Another descriptive explanation can be equally effective. The attorney needs to determine what description, if any, of the burden of proof ought to be explained. In court trials, arbitrations, and administrative hearings the burden of proof does not need to be explained. However, the law may be woven into the argument. For example, the advocate may say: "We have proved every essential element in this matter by a preponderance of the evidence. We have proved that what we said happened, really did happen."

Example

In this case, we have the burden of proof—the burden of proving our case to you. The judge will tell you—and now I am quoting from what the court will read to you later in this case—"The party that has the burden of proof must persuade you by the evidence that the claim is more probably true than not true and that it outweighs the evidence opposed to it." Now that is the law.

As the plaintiff, our proof must outweigh the defendant's proof. The phrase, "preponderance of the evidence," means nothing more than the greater weight of the evidence, the greater likelihood of the truth. To prove our case all we have to do is to tip the scales in our favor. It may help you to visualize in your mind the scales of justice. One side of the scale holds the evidence of my injured client, Dennis Burdock; the other scale holds the evidence of the defendant bicycle manufacturer—Schwann. Little Dennis Burdock doesn't have to topple the scales. He just has to tip them in his favor. All we have to do is tip those scales by the weight of the evidence, slightly in our favor, and we have carried our burden of proof.

3.62 Comment on Liability and Damages

A plaintiff in a civil case may prefer to argue damages after explaining the basis for liability. The defense may prefer to argue against damages initially in the closing argument and then argue the lack of liability on the part of the defense. This approach reduces the awkwardness of having to explain the possibility of damages after arguing the plaintiff has no right to recovery.

Example (Defense Case)

Dennis Burdock is a brain-damaged child who will need constant medical care and supervision. His condition is irreparable. This is a terrible tragedy. But Schwann, the maker of the bicycle, isn't responsible. Dennis was too small for the bike his grandparents bought him. His own parents never took the bike into a dealer to have the seat adjusted. Dennis' bike did not malfunction. Dennis was too small a child to control that bike. And Dennis' parents knew it.

3.63 Describe the Award of Damages

The advocate for the plaintiff may need to explain why damages should be awarded to reimburse the plaintiff for the injuries suffered, income lost, or expenses incurred.

Example

A long time ago people were guided by the law of retribution in these matters. The law was to do to another what he did to you and your family. You may have heard it expressed as: "an eye for an eye, a tooth for a tooth, blow for blow." But with the development of our system of justice, we have become more civilized. We do not ask that the defendant be hurt. All we ask is he fairly compensate the plaintiff for the wrong done with money damages. Why money damages? Because it is the only answer the law provides. There is no other alternative than this.

3.64 Summarize the Amount of Damages

The argument may contain a request for a specific amount of damages to be awarded with an explanation for the amount of money sought. Asking for a specified amount of damages is usually much more effective than leaving the assessment to the fact finder. There are some cases where a request for a general amount of damages as part of the verdict may be effective, but usually the better strategy is to request an amount of money or a range of amounts.

Example (Actual Damages)

And now, (pointing to chart), here is a list of the damages Janice Harper has suffered. Your responsibility is to determine the amount of damages the defendant must rightfully pay to Ms. Harper because she lost her leg. It is up to you to determine the amount of damages Ms. Harper is rightfully entitled to as a result of the negligence of the defendant. The defendant's negligence prevents her from leading a full and complete life, and prevents her from continuing her lifelong dream of being a professional dancer. I will go through each of these types of damages and explain why each is a reasonable amount of money Ms. Harper has a right to receive:

The severity of the injury and disability	$250,000.00
Loss of past earnings	$30,000.00
Loss of future earnings	$600,000.00
Past medical expenses	$85,000.00
Future medical expenses	$45,000.00
Disfigurement and inability to walk	$500,000.00
Past pain and suffering	$100,000.00
Future pain and suffering	$250,000.00
TOTAL	$1,860,000.00

This total of $1,860,000 is a substantial amount of money, but just think of the substantial pain endured by Ms. Harper, the substantial loss of her professional career, and her substantial personal loss.

Example (Intangible Damages)

The tragedy in this case is that Timmy and Carol will never see their mom again. She died under the wheels of the defendant's truck. The further tragedy is that there is no way that Ms. Bachmeier can be brought back to life to live with her children. As I mentioned before, the only thing our society allows to compensate Timmy and Carol for the loss of their mother is money damages. In this jurisdiction, the judge will tell you Timmy and Carol are entitled to receive an award of damages for the loss of the love and affection of their mother, for the loss of never being able to love, hug, be held by, laugh with, cry with, and just be with, their mother. You have to decide how much to award Timmy and Carol. How does one assess the loss of the love and affection of a mother? How does one put a dollar amount on such a terrible loss? Sometimes, stories about life help us determine the value of life. This story might help you determine the value of a lost mother.

This story requires us to go back in time, before this tragedy. Imagine that Timmy and Carol are on vacation with their mom along the ocean. Mom relaxes on the beach, and Timmy and Carol tell her they are going to go for a walk down the beach looking for shells. They walk about a block down the beach, and Carol stumbles over something in the sand. She looks down and sees something silver gleaming. Timmy says "What's that?" Carol says "Let's find out." And they begin to dig around this gleaming silver object. When they finish digging, Carol says "You know what this looks like? This looks like one of those magic genie lamps." And Timmy says "You mean one of those lamps you rub and a genie appears and grants your wishes?" And Carol says "I'm going to find out. I'm going to rub it." And so she rubs it, and magically a genie appears and says to them, "Today, Timmy and Carol, is your very lucky day. You have released me from the magic lamp and I am going to reward you by giving you two million dollars." You can imagine how excited Timmy and Carol are. They hug each other and Timmy says to Carol, "Mom will be so thrilled!" "Aaaahhh," the genie interrupts, "There is one condition. I will give you two million dollars, but you see your mother over there lying on the beach—you will never, ever see her again." Now, I ask you, members of the Jury, do you think Timmy and Carol would consider for one moment taking two million dollars or any amount of money and never see, hug, and love their mom ever again?

Example (Punitive Damages)

The judge is going to tell you that you may award punitive damages in this case if you find the conduct of the defendant wanton and willful and in gross disregard for the safety of others. The law allows you to award punitive damages in this case to punish the defendant. An award of punitive damages allows you to take away some money from the defendant to make the defendant and other future defendants know this should not happen ever again. An award of punitive damages is not made to the plaintiff to give him something because he deserves it, but rather it is to act as a deterrence—that is, to send the message to the defendant and other future defendants not to do this in the future.

To send this message, the amount of punitive damages must be significant. The amount must be enough so the defendants feel they are punished. How do you set that amount of damages? It depends on who the defendant is, how much of a profit it makes, and how much it is worth.

The defendant here is a corporation that is worth 60 million dollars and has average profits of 6 million dollars a year. Those are staggering amounts of money. And only a staggering amount of punitive damages will affect the defendant and have an impact on its future conduct. If you took away from it 3 million dollars—one half of one year's profit— the defendant would be properly punished under law. And when you consider how wanton, how willful, and how grossly indifferent it was to the safety of the plaintiff and others, you may conclude that even 3 million dollars is not enough money to fairly punish the defendant corporation.

3.65 Propose a Per Diem Argument

A "per diem" argument, which divides a period of time into small units and assesses a dollar value for each of these units is one way to calculate damages. For example, if a party will suffer permanent injuries for the remaining thirty years of life, the plaintiff's advocate might argue the plaintiff is entitled to receive $100 a day for thirty years because of this continuing injury, for a total of $1,095,000. Many jurisdictions prohibit per diem arguments. Other jurisdictions permit the argument to be used by the plaintiff's advocate as an alternative way to determine certain damages.

Example

How do you arrive at dollar amounts for the intangible things—for pain and suffering? You have heard the testimony about the pain the plaintiff has suffered in this case. How do you determine how much to compensate the plaintiff for that pain? If a person goes to a dentist to have a cavity filled, the dentist might say, "I can drill your tooth without any novocaine or any painkiller, but for an additional $30 I can give you novocaine, and you will be free from pain for one hour. $30 for freedom from pain for 60 minutes." Who would refuse to pay $30 for freedom for one hour from such excruciating pain?

3.66 Do Not Comment on the Financial Status of Party

The general rule is that the financial status of a party is irrelevant and cannot be referred to during summation, unless the financial status is an issue in a case. For example, if punitive damages are sought, the financial status of a defendant will be relevant because the assessment of punitive damages depends upon the financial status of the party.

3.67 Explain the Impact of Tax Laws

If the amount of the decision is not taxable income, then the general rule is that tax law cannot be mentioned during summation. In some cases, the tax laws will have an effect upon the decision and can be mentioned.

3.68 Do Not Refer to Insurance

The general rule is that neither party may refer to the existence or non-existence of insurance during a case, and this rule includes summation. Insurance may only be mentioned if its existence is an issue in the case. The rules of evidence prohibit references to liability insurance. See Fed.Rule of Evid. 412.

L. HOW TO DELIVER THE SUMMATION

The more effective and persuasive an advocate is in presenting a closing argument, the greater the chance a favorable determination will be reached. If the evidence presented in a case is weak, the advocate will have little chance of convincing the decision maker in final argument. If the evidence presented during the case is strong, statements made during summation will most likely match the conclusions the decision maker has already reached. If, however, the evidence presented by both sides is balanced, the closing argument becomes vitally important and may have a significant influence in the determination made.

Many of the factors that influence the presentation of an opening statement also affect summation. Factors such as confidence, sincerity, interest, honesty, dress, demeanor, voice, tone, use of simple language, and selection of impact words will affect the persuasiveness of the closing argument.

3.69 Stand

The advocate needs to present the summation from a position that enhances its presentation. In general, the more effective location is to stand in front of the decision maker and not hidden behind a lectern or table.

In some forums, local rules require the advocate stand behind a lectern when presenting the closing argument. In these situations, the advocate should ask permission to stand away from the lectern in order to make a more effective presentation. If this request is denied, the advocate may use visual aids and exhibits which permit the advocate to stand away from the lectern or by the easel which holds the visual aid and which can be placed in front of the decision maker.

If a lectern must be used, it may be used as a tool, and all the effective communication techniques can be applied with the restrictions that a lectern places on such things as movement and gestures. A lectern may also provide a safe refuge for those who are uncomfortable with or have not had the time to practice speaking away from a table or lectern. It is too easy, however, to overuse notes while at a lectern or to use no gestures and remain frozen in one spot, which causes both the advocate and argument to be boring.

3.70 Move

Movement can be effective during summation. The advocate can provide the decision maker with a different view. Movement and stance must be orchestrated so as not to be distracting. Movement that appears random and purposeless should be avoided. Movement should be used for transitions or to make a point more emphatically. Some forums do not allow movement; some court and hearing rooms may not permit movement. In these cases, do not move, or try not to.

3.71 Maintain Appropriate Distance

The advocate must maintain an appropriate distance from the decision maker. The distance that an advocate maintains should be flexible and vary in different circumstances. During most of the closing argument, the advocate should maintain a distance of between three to eight feet. Periodically, the advocate can move closer to the decision maker, if appropriate and possible.

In a jury trial, the advocate must avoid making a juror uncomfortable by being too close. One way to avoid this is to stand at the jury rail between two jurors and make eye contact with only the jurors in the back row, saving eye contact with the front row for the approach to and movement away from this brief, close presentation. An advocate should observe the jurors' reactions and move closer when appropriate and stand further away when necessary to avoid making jurors feel uncomfortable.

3.72 Gesture

Appropriate gestures should be used during summation to make the presentation more interesting. A lack of gestures or use of awkward hand movements or wild gesticulations should be avoided. Firm and purposeful gestures should be used, and those gestures should appear natural.

3.73 Look and Listen

One of the most effective ways to be persuasive and compelling is to look the decision makers directly in the eyes during summation. This also helps hold their attention, and allows the advocate to observe their reactions. Eye contact does not mean staring at or looking at decision makers so intensely that they become uneasy.

3.74 Use Transitions

The closing argument is more effective if the attorney employs transitions between both major and minor subjects during the presentation. Preparatory remarks, silence, a louder voice, a softer voice, visual aids, movement and gestures are all ways to make a transition.

3.75 Develop Your Own Style

The final argument must be delivered in a style that reflects the advocate's abilities. An advocate should avoid copying and mimicking another person's style but should be open to adapting and reworking what someone else has done if this style appears effective. Many parts of a closing argument may be taken from previous arguments or presentations made by other attorneys because of the similarity of the cases, the issues, or the quality of the ideas.

3.76 Observe the Decision Maker's Reaction

The advocate must observe the decision maker's reactions during the closing argument and consider these reactions during the argument. The facial expressions, body language, and eye contact displayed communicate some information about attitude or position. These perceptions may not always be accurate. Because it is difficult to determine accurately what people are thinking just by watching them during a presentation, care must be taken not to overreact and not to completely change an approach because of what may be a mistakenly perceived reaction.

3.77 Prepare Notes and Outlines

It will be necessary in many cases for an advocate to rely upon notes or an outline during closing argument to ensure all important points have been covered. The longer the closing argument the more likely the need to rely on notes. An advocate should never read a prepared closing argument or follow the notes so closely that eye contact is not established. Reading the argument usually leads to a very boring and uninteresting presentation. Occasional references to notes are appropriate as long as such references do not unreasonably interfere with or detract from the presentation.

Prepared outlines can be effectively used in summation if combined with the use of visual aids. A prepared diagram, a blackboard, a whiteboard, easel paper, or an overhead transparency may contain an outline of part or all of the closing which highlights important matters and assists in explaining the argument.

M. COMPLEX CASES

3.78 Summation in Complex Cases

Complex cases present a challenge to the advocate in summation. The task will be to summarize the massive amount of information in an understandable and persuasive way. At the end of the summation the decision maker should readily understand what needs to be decided and why these issues should be decided in favor of the party represented by the advocate.

The best structure for a summation will depend upon the type of complex case and the positions asserted by the party. In a jury trial, the special interrogatories may provide an outline for summation. In other cases, the factual and legal issues to be decided may provide a useful outline.

Time restrictions are typically placed upon summation in complex cases. The amount of time available will determine what can be presented, and the advocate will need to be very selective in deciding what to cover.

The significance of the issues and the amount of resources available will usually permit the use of visual aids during summation. Exhibits used during the case may be summarized. Visual aids including diagrams, charts, overhead transparencies, and computer generated presentations can be prepared and used. Consultants with experience in the areas can be retained to create visual aids.

The use of creative efforts in complex cases can also be very effective. In addition to history, anecdotes, poems, books, and stories to make a point, movies can also be used. A videotape can be created consisting of evidence presented during the case and scenes from a movie which relate to the theory of a case. The videotape can summarize the testimony and exhibits and show a movie scene which highlights the point. In one case, a plaintiff's attorney relied on the theory that the defendants were repeatedly warned of an upcoming event but continually ignored the warnings, causing injury to the plaintiff. The attorney created a videotape which showed evidence in the case of unheeded warnings and which showed scenes from the movie Titanic of ship officers negligently ignoring warnings. The point of the visual aid was to persuade the jurors that the defendants failed to heed obvious warnings which caused plaintiff to suffer a disaster.

N. WHAT YOU CANNOT DO

The advocate is generally allowed wide latitude in discussing the evidence and presenting theories during summation. Objections may be asserted during closing argument to prevent improper statements and conclusion.

If there is an opportunity for a closing argument or rebuttal after the opposition, the advocate may prefer not to object but later comment on an inappropriate statement made by the opposition. If an advocate has no follow-up summation, an objection may be necessary to repair any damage and to preserve a matter for appeal. Many advocates do not object during final argument unless the opponent is saying or doing something that is clearly improper and unfairly prejudicial to the case.

An objection to improper summation must be made in a timely fashion. Usually, the objection must be made immediately during or at the end of the summation. In a jury trial, the objecting attorney should also request a curative instruction. The trial judge may then attempt to reduce the prejudicial impact of the improper comments by instructing the jurors to disregard the comments. Some jurisdictions require the attorney to make the objection as well as request a curative instruction. The reason for the curative instruction is to provide an opportunity for the trial judge to rectify the error. The damage done by some improper comments may not be correctable by a curative instruction.

Appellate courts have reversed verdicts and granted new trials even where the trial judge gave curative instructions because the comments were so prejudicial as to deny the objecting party a fair jury trial. For example, comments made by an attorney regarding the existence of insurance in a civil jury trial may be impossible to correct. Further, improper comments made in a jury trial in which the issues are very close may be sufficient to support a motion for a mistrial. The facts and circumstances of each case determine whether the impropriety of the remarks is incurable. Appellate courts may reverse a verdict without objections being made to the closing argument where the substantial interests of justice require such a reversal. However, the granting of a new trial or an appellate court reversal for improper closing argument seldom occurs. New hearings or reversals based on improper argument do not occur in court trials and administrative hearings as the judge can sort out and ignore improper argument and make a decision on the facts and law.

The following paragraphs describe objections that may be made to improper comments during summation to correct or reduce the impact of the errors.

3.79 Argue New Matters

An advocate may not introduce or argue new matters during closing argument beyond the scope of admitted evidence. References to facts or to the law which go beyond the evidence or legal issues are objectionable. References to evidence which is inadmissible or to facts and opinions that were not introduced during the trial or hearing are also improper.

Objection:

> Counsel is improperly referring to matters not presented in this case.

Response to Objection:

> Explain the evidence or law that supports the comments made.
>
> Avoid referring to inadmissible or unproven evidence.
>
> Hope the judge and opposition have poor memories.

3.80 Misstate the Evidence

Misstating evidence is improper. An objection can be made if the evidence is mischaracterized.

In a jury trial, the judge may not recall the exact evidence or may permit the attorney broad latitude in characterizing the evidence because the judge has given or will give an instruction that what the attorneys say during summation is not evidence. The jurors will be instructed that they are to rely upon their own recollection of the evidence. In some cases, the judge may give a curative instruction during summation advising the jury to ignore an improper characterization made by the attorney.

In cases where the advocate makes a misstatement regarding a critical matter, the opposition may ask the judge to refer to the transcript of the trial (if available) to determine the propriety of the statement. It will be very difficult or impossible for the court reporter to locate an exact reference to evidence from stenographic notes without prior notice.

Misstatements of evidence may also occur regarding evidence admitted for a limited purpose. During argument, the advocate might use evidence admitted for one purpose to prove something else. An objection should be made to this improper characterization.

Objection:

The evidence presented during the trial is misstated.

Response to Objection:

Explain the source of evidence supporting the comment.

Explain the comment is a permissible inference that may be drawn from the facts presented.

Argue the statement is a good faith belief of what the evidence was.

Explain that you have a real poor memory.

3.81 Make an Improper Legal Argument

The advocate may not argue a personal interpretation of the law applicable to the case. It is proper to correctly explain the applicable law and apply it to the facts. It is improper to misstate or misinterpret the law.

Objection:

The law is being incorrectly stated.

Response to Objection:

Refer to the precise language of the law.

Argue the explanation is a fair interpretation of the law as applied to the facts.

Admit to the judge you never understood the rules in school.

3.82 Make an Improper Personal Argument

An advocate may not state a personal viewpoint or make personal remarks about the facts, credibility of witnesses, expert opinions, or other evidence. For example, the advocate may not say: "There is no question in my mind that the plaintiff lied to you. I heard what you heard, and I saw what you saw. I am convinced the plaintiff lied." A prosecutor may not state: "I have prosecuted over 20 drug dealers over the years. I have never been as sure as I am in this case about the guilt of the defendant. I not only think he is guilty, but I firmly believe as an officer of the court that he is guilty as charged." While an inadvertent, occasional use of a statement prefaced by "I believe" may not call for an objection, a serious deliberate effort to express and rely on personal opinion should call for an objection.

Objection:

The opposition is stating improper personal opinions.

Response to Objection:

Avoid making statements of personal opinion.

Avoid using the word "I" in a statement referring to an opinion or conclusion.

Preface such remarks with:

"It is clear from the evidence . . . ."

"The only conclusion that can be reached is . . . ."

3.83 Make an Improper "Golden Rule" Argument

The "Golden Rule" argument is a statement asking the decision makers to put themselves in the place of a party or witness. An example is "Put yourself in the place of the defendant in this case. How would you want yourself to be treated?" The decision makers are to decide the case based on the facts, not based upon how they personally want to be treated as a party or believed as a witness.

Objection:

The advocate is improperly asking the decision makers to put themselves in the place of a party.

Response to Objection:

Avoid making this statement.

Ask the decision makers to rely upon their common sense or how a reasonable person would respond and not how they personally would respond.

Hire an alchemist.

3.84 Appeal to Passion

Statements are improper if they serve only to inflame passions. Advocates may legitimately invoke emotions in a case, but may not rely on improper sympathy. The drama inherent in many cases will naturally result in appropriate emotional closing arguments. Empathy, sadness, and tears may naturally result from the atmosphere of the case. Overstated emotion and improper appeals to passion and sympathy are not only improper, they frequently are ineffectual and offend the fact finder.

Objection:

Counsel is appealing to passion.

Response to Objection:

Explain the emotions are a natural part of the trial.

Present the argument in a less emotional manner.

Hide the onion you used.

3.85 Appeal to Prejudice

It is a gross violation of the fundamental precepts of our system to appeal to the prejudices or biases regarding racial, sexist, economic, religious, political, or similar arguments. These comments are not only unconscionable but are also grounds for substantial ethical sanctions.

Example

Whatever doubts you may have about the defendant's liability in this case can be resolved by considering the wealth of the defendant. This very rich and well-off defendant can clearly afford to pay the plaintiff a lot of money and should be made to do so, even if you aren't sure the defendant is negligent.

Objection:

The advocate is basing the argument on prejudice.

Response to Objection:

Don't ever do this. Don't even think about ever doing it.

3.86 Make Other Improper Comments

The following statements represent examples of other improper comments: mentioning insurance, referring to the financial status of a party unless punitive damages are in issue, implying that the fact finders as taxpayers would ultimately be responsible for a damage award to a plaintiff who sued a governmental agency, telling the fact finders that the present case is not the first time litigants have asked for such damages, comments that denounce or degrade the opponent or the adverse party, a comparison between the resources of the opposing sides, and any other unprofessional statements.

Objection:

The opponent has made an improper and prejudicial comment.

Response to Objection:

> Look deservedly ashamed and take your lumps.
>
> Go for counseling after the case.

3.87 Make Improper References to the Invocation of a Privilege or Unavailable Evidence

All jurisdictions recognize evidentiary privileges which prevent the introduction of relevant information. These jurisdictions differ regarding whether opposing counsel may suggest that the decision maker draw adverse inferences from the invocation of such a privilege. For example, in jurisdictions that recognize marital privileges and prevent spouses from testifying to confidential marital communications, references to the excluded marital conversation may not be made and the decision maker may not be asked to draw the inference that what was discussed must be harmful to the case.

In some cases, relevant evidence cannot be obtained by a party for legitimate reasons. The evidence may have been inadvertently lost by a third party. A key witness may not be able to be located after substantial efforts. Some evidence may be outside the reach of subpoena power. In many jurisdictions, it is improper to ask that adverse inferences be drawn from the failure of the other side to introduce such evidence.

Objection:

> The opponent is improperly drawing adverse inferences from the lawful invocation of a privilege.

Response to Objection:

> Check the laws of the jurisdiction to determine whether this is permissible before doing it. If it is, provide the citation to the permitting authority.
>
> Make a reference to the missing evidence without drawing any adverse inferences.
>
> Next time hire Paul Drake and Della Street.

3.88 Is There a Proper Scope of Argument?

The scope of rebuttal has limitations. Rebuttal evidence is admissible only to rebut new evidence introduced by the opponent either through cross-examination or in direct examination during the opponent's own case. Rebuttal evidence going beyond this limitation is not admissible.

Objection:

> The argument exceeds the proper scope of the rebuttal argument.

Response to Objection:

> Explain to the judge the topics raised by the opponent permit the rebuttal argument.

> Include the arguments during the initial summation and do not save them for rebuttal.

> Ask the judge to exercise discretion and permit a broader rebuttal.

> Explain with a straight face that your rebuttal rebuts the rebuttable parts of the rebutted argument.

3.89 What Prosecutors Cannot Do

In criminal cases, the prosecutor must be careful not to overstep the bounds of fair argument. Prosecutors may be bound by a higher standard than defense counsel. Defense counsel may rely on the constitutional rights of the defendant which protect against an over-zealous prosecutor. For example, it is a constitutional violation for a prosecutor to comment directly or indirectly on the defendant's failure to testify. It is also improper for a prosecutor to tell a jury that unless they bring in a conviction a lot of money will have been wasted in the case and that the defendant would not have been arrested if he was innocent.

Objection:

Prosecutor has made unfair prejudicial comments.

Response to Objection:

Do not make such statements.

Tone down the argument.

Become a defense lawyer.

3.90 Can These Be Interruptions?

Objections may not be made merely to interrupt the advocate and distract the decision maker. If an opponent makes such harassing objections, the advocate should object to the objections.

3.91 Admonishing Counsel, But Not You

If the opponent makes a number of improper comments or continues to make inappropriate comments after an objection has been sustained, the advocate should consider asking that the opponent be admonished.

3.92 Whining, Why Not?

It is improper to whine, grovel, or throw a tantrum during summation in an effort to win.

*

RESOURCES

Bibliography

Art of Advocacy, Lawrence J. Smith (M. Bender 1978–).

The Art of Summation, Melvin Block (New York State Association of Trial Lawyers 1964).

The Battle for Credibility: Establishing and Maintaining Credibility From Voir Dire to Closing Argument, Irwin Birnbaum, 20 *Trial* 76–78 (1984).

Closing Argument, Larry R. Feldman, 23 *Trial* 98 (1987).

Closing Argument, James R. Lucas, 21 Trial Lawyers Quarterly 19–33 (1990).

Closing Argument, Paul L. Redfearn, 57 *UMKC Law Review* 821–823 (1989).

Closing Argument, Jerome L. Ringler, 23 *Trial* 112 (1987).

Closing Argument (New York), Michael Paul Ringwood, 62 *New York State Bar Journal* 10 (1990).

Closing Argument: The Art and The Law, Jacob A. Stein (Callaghan 1969–).

Closing Argument: Consolidating Your Theme, Bob Gibbins, 26 *Trial* 83–88 (1990).

Closing Argument: Rhetorical Question, (Illinois), Theodore Postel, 136 *Chicago Daily Law Bulletin* 1 (1990).

Closing Argument: A Systematic Approach, James M. Thomas, 17 *Georgia State Bar Journal* 80–82 (1980).

Closing Argument a Time for Reality Check, Paul M. Lisnek, 139 *Chicago Daily Law Bulletin* 6 (1993).

Closing Argument in Civil Cases (Missouri), W. Dudley McCarter, 46 *Journal of the Missouri Bar* 31–41 (1990).

Closing Argument in a Criminal Case, Calvin Lee, 22 *Trial* 104 (1986).

Closing Argument Deemed an Admission of Liability (Illinois), Theodore Postel, 134 *Chicago Daily Law Bulletin* 1 (1988).

Closing Argument Procedure, J. Alexander Tanford, 10 *American Journal of Trial Advocacy* 47–140 (1986).

Closing Argument Procedure, J. Alexander Tanford, 37 *Defense Law Journal* 401–498 (1988).

Closing Argument Restrictions, Pamela A. Kuehn, 17 *Loyola of Los Angeles Law Review* 116 (1984).

Comment in Closing Argument Not Reversible Error, Jay Judge and James R. Schirott, 135 *Chicago Daily Law Bulletin* 3 (1988).

Use of Analogies in Closing Argument, James J. Eischen, Jr., 16 *Barrister* 53 (1989).

Special Interrogatory—Closing Argument (Illinois), Theodore Postel, 134 *Chicago Daily Law Bulletin* 1 (1988).

Judicial Admission: Closing Argument (Illinois), Theodore Postel, 136 *Chicago Daily Law Bulletin* 1 (1990).

Pain Analogies for Closing Argument, David R. Lee, 20 *Trial Lawyers Quarterly* 60–65 (1990).

Effective Closing Argument (book reviews), Peter C. Lagarias, rev. Neil Pedersen, 17 *Western State University Law Review* 235–237 (1989).

"Hard Blows" Versus "Foul Ones": Restrictions on Trial Counsel's Closing Argument, Randy V. Cargill, *Army Lawyer* 20–27 (1991).

Jury Argument: How to Prepare and Present a Closing Argument, Scott Baldwin, 20 *Trial* 58 (1984).

The Limits of Closing Argument in Florida: A Practitioner's Guide, Harold Oehler, 65 *Florida Bar Journal* 62–65 (1991).

One Closing Slip Can't Be "Fixed" By Another (closing argument), Robert E. Bartkus, 129 *New Jersey Law Journal* 1 (1991).

Opening Statement and Closing Argument: A Golden Opportunity and the Last Chance, David A. Handley, 34 *For the Defense* 16–21 (1992).

Oklahoma Law on Closing Argument, Keith N. Bystrom, 37 *Oklahoma Law Review* 445–494 (1984).

Prosecutorial Misconduct; Improper Remarks During Closing Argument, Frank D. Celebrezze, 23 *Trial* 54 (1987).

Winning Final Arguments, Minnesota Trial Lawyers Association (Minnesota Trial Lawyers Association 1981).

Video

Art of Advocacy Skills in Action Series: Summation, Matthew Bender & Co., Inc. (1981).

The Art of Advocacy: Strategies for Closing Arguments, National Institute For Trial Advocacy (1987).

Closing Arguments, Trial Preparation, Anderson Publishing (1990).

Closing Argument in a Civil Case I, National Institute For Trial Advocacy (1977–1980).

Closing Argument in a Civil Case II, National Institute For Trial Advocacy (1979).

Closing Argument in a Civil Case III, National Institute For Trial Advocacy (1977–1980).

Closing Argument in a Criminal Case I, National Institute For Trial Advocacy (1977–1980).

Closing Argument in a Criminal Case II, National Institute For Trial Advocacy (1977–1980).

Closing Argument in a Criminal Case III, National Institute For Trial Advocacy (1977–1980).

Closing Arguments in a Contract Action, Part One, National Institute For Trial Advocacy (1987).

Closing Arguments in a Contract Action, Part Two, National Institute For Trial Advocacy (1987).

Closing Arguments in a Products Liability Case, Part One, National Institute For Trial Advocacy (1987).

Closing Arguments in a Products Liability Case, Part Two, National Institute For Trial Advocacy (1987).

Film

Class Action (1991).

Music Box (1989).

The Verdict (1982).

To Kill a Mockingbird (1962).

Inherit the Wind (1960).

Adam's Rib (1949).

INDEX

Discovery,
    Complex cases, Bk.1 § 2.40
Discretionary review, petitions for, Bk.1 § 4.27.5
Disqualification of judge, Bk.1 § 2.20
    For cause, Bk.1 § 2.21
    Without cause, Bk.1 § 2.22
Doctor-patient privilege, Bk.4 § 2.18.2
Document hearings,
    Arbitration proceedings, Bk.1 § 3.12
Document management system,
    Complex cases, Bk.1 § 2.38
    Disclosure of documents, Bk.1 § 2.38
    Marking documents, Bk.1 § 2.38
Documents,
    Admissibility, Bk.4 Ch.2 E
    Best evidence rule, Bk.4 § 2.25
    Depository, Bk.1 § 2.39
    Duplicates, Bk.4 § 2.25
    Foundation, Bk.4 § 4.21
    Management in complex cases, Bk.1 § 2.38
    Motion documents, Bk.1 § 3.56
    Original writings, Bk.4 § 2.25
    Parol evidence rule, Bk.4 § 2.27
    Self-authenticating documents, Bk.4 § 4.19
Dying declaration, Bk.4 § 3.22
    Fed.R.Evid. 803(b)(2), Bk.4 § 3.22
Effective advocacy techniques, Bk.1 Ch. 3 D
Errors,
    Types and degree of error, Bk.1 § 4.23
      Harmless error, Bk.1 § 4.23.2
      Plain error, Bk.1 § 4.23.3
      Prejudicial error, Bk.1 § 4.23.1; Bk.4 § 1.47
Ethics,
    Duties,
      Abide by client's decisions, Bk.1 § 1.38.1
      Competent representation, Bk.1 § 1.38.2
      Confidentiality, Bk.1 § 1.38.3
      Conflict of interest rule, Bk.1 § 1.38.4
      Disclosure of controlling authority, Bk.1 § 1.38.8
      Evidentiary considerations, Bk.1 § 1.38.7
      Expedite the case, Bk.1 § 1.38.6
      Fulfill obligations, Bk.1 § 1.38.10
      Good faith, Bk.1 § 1.38.5
    Misconduct, Bk.1 § 1.38.11
    Model Rules of Professional Conduct, Bk.1 § 1.38
    Personal ethics, Bk.1 § 1.38
    Professional ethics, Bk.1 § 1.38
    Standard of conduct, Bk.1 § 1.38.5